LIVING BEYOND *The Box*

NELSON L. NOGGLE, PH.D.

authorHOUSE®

AuthorHouse™
1663 Liberty Drive
Bloomington, IN 47403
www.authorhouse.com
Phone: 1 (800) 839-8640

Published by AuthorHouse   12/21/2015

ISBN: 978-1-4817-0931-6 (sc)
ISBN: 978-1-5049-6553-8 (hc)
ISBN: 978-1-4817-0932-3 (e)

Library of Congress Control Number: 2015920792

Print information available on the last page.

CONTENTS

ACKNOWLEDGEMENTS

This book, **_Living Beyond The Box_**, was not possible without the help and encouragement from many people and especially from God's Holy Spirit. I want to acknowledge especially the following people …

My Wife, Karen Noggle. Karen provided ideas, editorial comments, productive criticism, resources and patience throughout the entire period of writing and revising manuscript. Thank you, Karen, you are wonderful! You are my "Geel" …

My Illustrator, Emily Krause. Emily saved the day, as she created each of the illustrations found in this book. Her creativity and characterizations helped immensely to continue my reliance upon visuals to advance the concepts therein.

My Family – my mother Catherine Noggle, father Wayne Noggle, daughter Tammy Raynor, son Josh Noggle, grandchildren Kevin, Eric, Luke, Andrew, Bryan, Tina, Marianne, Katie, Becky and Rita, as well as grandparents, aunts, uncles, cousins, and in-laws.

My Close Friends and Colleagues – Hank Suverkrup, John Harrold, Donald Thoren, Kerry Ugalde Hyatt, Betty Campbell Henderson, Mark LaScola, Claudia Murphy, Sorrel Bowman Rogers, Carmen de la Torre,

Donald Freeman, Jackie Garner, Rosemary King, Linda Carmichael Gibson, Richard Hendrix, plus the entire staff members of the Phoenix Young Fathers Program, the Phoenix Big Brothers/Sisters Program, the Arizona Parents Anonymous Program, and the Arizona Drug and Alcohol Prevention programs [just to name some of the programs that relied on *The Box* in some way. But the list goes on, all the teachers, students, coworkers, clients and customers I encountered throughout my school and work experiences.

I have been blessed all along the way by contributions from others, and grateful that I was able to 'wake up" one day to the notion that if I'm going learn, I must do so for the right reasons – for the intrinsic and functional value of the actual knowledge, skills and capabilities to be learned. In a sense, I finally began to take myself out of *The Box*. I was 27 years old when this transformation really began to occur.

THE AUTHOR

Nelson L. Noggle, Ph.D.

CENTERS FOR THE ADVANCEMENT OF
EDUCATIONAL PRACTICES

CAEP

I am a parent, educator and researcher who has worked with hundreds of educational programs, schools and social agencies as well as thousands of parents and counselors. I taught at the elementary, secondary and university levels. For the past 30 years, my focus has been on understanding how adults motivate children, youth and other adults, especially how they motivate them to learn.

What I discovered was pretty simple ...

- ❏ *People at any age learn very little, unless they <u>aim to learn</u>.*
- ❏ *Learning is both a process and an outcome, and requires <u>self-motivation</u>.*

As a result, I founded the *Centers for the Advancement of Educational Practices (CAEP),* a small educational services firm dedicated to the continuous improvement of the methods that parents, educators, counselors and managers use to bring about learning. The two main thrusts of the *CAEP Mission* are as follows:

- ❏ *Freeing people to learn, in any setting!*
- ❏ *Serving those who are serving learners!*

During my early work, *The Box* and several other visual models became useful tools for those wanting to know how to motivate people to learn. Since then, I have used those models to train thousands of parents, teachers, counselors and managers. This book was written for those who would like to apply many of the principles and ideas surrounding *The Box* in their everyday lives. There are two goals that drove the writing of this book.

❑ *The primary goal is to free you to live and learn beyond **The Box**.*
❑ *The secondary goal is to help you free others to live and learn beyond **The Box**.*

Our parents had the huge responsibility of educating us as children and youth. Extended family members, friends, church members and other members of the community also tried to help us to learn. There are many professionals who also tackled the job of educating us, such as teachers, counselors, social workers, and creators of learning programs and materials. Part of the struggle for our parents was how to guarantee that the approach and content of all that teaching would remain appropriate for us, not to mention also trying to control the impact of television, movies, music, magazines and the internet and social media.

This book is designed help us gain a perspective on how our parents, teachers and counselors impacted us as children and youth – to help us see if we ended up *living in The Box*. It is also designed to help us look at ourselves today so that we can learn to *live beyond The Box*.

This book should help parents, educators, counselors and leaders who manage the efforts of others. It should help them to understand their job in terms of *The Box* they and their constituents find themselves in at any given time. After all, learning is a life-long mission requiring a lot of motivation and effort. The question is, "Who is responsible to motivate us?"

What is truly unique about this book is how it uses visual models to guide you as you try to become more self-motivated and self-assured -- such as those designed to:

- ❑ *Understand **The Box***
- ❑ *Become aware of the consequences of **The Box***
- ❑ *Sense how **The Box** has played and currently plays a role in your life*
- ❑ *Learn ways to use **The Box** in an appropriate manner*
- ❑ *Learn ways to then **Live Beyond The Box***

UNDERSTANDING *The Box*

LIFE IS HUMOROUS

It is almost a "scream" when we see someone getting in over their heads as if they "can't wait to get there". We want to yell, "Watch out!"

When we see the whole picture, if we look closely, we can see them headed into trouble carrying trouble with them. Yep, we get ourselves into all kinds of boxed-in situations, but we also arm ourselves with the ability to box others in as well.

It is hilarious to watch the roller-coaster-like and relentless pursuit of finding the right box and winning both in it and with it at the same time. Yet, as humorous as it looks to others, it looks even funnier as we become deadly serious in chasing down our victory in ***The Box***.

Nelson L. Noggle, Ph.D.

INTRODUCING *The Box*

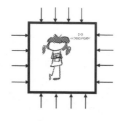

Children/youth and youth can get "boxed in" by all the things they are told to do and all the methods used to get them to do those things.

Being in a Box is part real and part perception

Adults, also, can get "boxed in" by all the things they are told to do and all the methods used to get them to do those things.

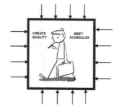

Children/youth can get *"boxed in"* by all the things they are told to do and all the methods used to get them to do those things. It is easy for parents to over-protect or over-control their children/youth, and to basically use the same methods at later ages they used when the kids were younger. Teachers are taught to use various behavior modification techniques, such as "assertive discipline" (etc.), primarily to control those students who are fairly undisciplined -- unfortunately it imprisons those who might be more easily motivated by other means. Their peers also use similar methods to attract and control them. For some, the feeling of being boxed-in comes from abusive forms of power and guilt used to force compliance.

Freedom is one of the growing needs of youth and adults. A steady diet or abusive forms of over-protection or over-control are extremely stressful and can lead to high feelings of *victimization,* which causes many to suffer in adulthood. I feel that God revealed **The Box** to me as a visual model for looking at what impacts the motivation of learners – children, youth and adults. He revealed it to me as I tried to help parents and teachers of **Head Start** children.

4

❑ ***The Box** is not bad in and of itself.*
❑ *A steady diet or abusive forms of **The Box** are harmful.*
❑ *Victimized thinking and co-dependencies result from too much of **The Box**.*
❑ *Our lives can get "**Boxed In**" by our own victimized thinking.*
❑ *We need strategies to **cope with and get beyond The Box**.*

The early pages of this book define ***The Box*** and discuss the various implications of its use. You will be able to assess how much it plays a part in your life, including how you react to it as well as how you rely on it to control situations and others – as a parent, teacher, leader or counselor. Later pages will give your ideas and strategies for ***living beyond The Box***.

LIFE IS HUMOROUS

Getting boxed-in happens to young and old alike. We often hear young people say, "I can't wait until I grow up so I can be my own boss". We want to scream at them that they will run the risk of becoming their own worst enemy.

BOSS SPELLED BACKWARD IS A DOUBLE SOB!

It doesn't matter what age we happen to be, we can become boxed-in by others and by ourselves. Living beyond **The Box** is all part of our persistent desire for freedom. Wars, big and small, are fought over the desire for freedom. Yet, we giggle as we escape **The Box** and yet we tend to put others in it.

It is outright fun to gain power over someone else, especially if they have had power over us – kids versus parents, students versus teachers, employees versus management, small versus big, poor versus rich, and ultimately me versus them.

DIRECTIONS

DIRECTIONS

➤ Someone tells us what to do or not to do
➤ Someone tells us what we did or did not do
➤ Someone gestures what to do or where to go
➤ Someone gives us detailed instructions on what to do or where to go
➤ Someone requires eye contact from us while giving directions
➤ Someone continues to watch and direct us while we try to perform

Much of parenting is like directing a play

The first dimension of *The Box* is called **DIRECTIONS**. This is when our parents, teachers and bosses told us what, how, when or where to do things. For example:

❑ Someone told us to clean up before doing something else we wanted to do

❑ Someone told us what looked alright and what did not look well enough

❑ Someone pointed to the things needing to be cleaned up and frowned

❑ Someone told us specifically what had to be cleaned up

❑ Someone told us to look them in the eye while they told us what to clean up

❑ Someone checked on our progress continually and told us what else to do

❑ And so forth – directing what we were to do

Recall a particular time when you were growing up when it felt as though someone was telling you what to do all the time. Try to remember how it felt. Did situations like this happen often?

<u>Write a brief description of those directions back then, and how you felt:</u>

<u>Now write a brief description of directions you were given recently, and how you felt:</u>

REWARDS

DIRECTIONS

➢ Someone promises us some type of material or fun reward for doing it

➢ Someone gives us some type of material or fun reward for doing it

➢ Someone provides some type of positive gestures or words for doing it

➢ Someone brags to others about what we did

➢ When we got away with it if we did not do it as directed

REWARDS

It is great looking for something nice to happen

The second dimension of ***The Box*** is called **REWARDS**. These are the things our parents, teachers and bosses promised and/or gave us for <u>doing</u> whatever it was they told us to do. For example:

❑ Someone promised us a grab-bag prize for doing our homework

❑ Someone gave us a grab-bag prize for doing our homework

❑ Someone praised us and smiled at us for doing our homework

❑ Someone bragged to other students about our doing our homework

❑ Someone offered us special privileges if we would do our homework

❑ And so forth – if you do that, you will get this

Recall times when you were growing up when you <u>did and did not</u> get an important reward when you were trying to do something someone wanted you to do. Try to remember how each time felt. Did this happen often?

<u>Write a brief description of what getting and not getting rewards felt like:</u>

<u>Does it still happen a lot now in your life? Write additional thoughts:</u>

PUNISHMENT

REWARDS

DIRECTIONS

PUNISHMENT

➤ Someone threatens some type of punishment if we do not do what is directed

➤ Someone punishes us for not doing it or doing it wrong

➤ Someone frowns, criticizes, spanks, suspends privileges, withholds rewards, etc.

➤ Someone embarrasses us by telling others what was not done or done wrong

Much of what we all worry about is punitive

The third dimension of ***The Box*** is called ***PUNISHMENT.*** These are the things our parents, teachers and bosses threatened and/or administered to us for <u>not doing</u> whatever it was they told us to do, or for <u>doing it wrong</u>. For example:

❑ Someone threatened that we could not go play if we did not clean up our room

❑ Someone grounded us from our friends for the day because we did a poor job

❑ Someone frowned and criticized our poor work as they punished us

❑ Someone told our friends and their parents why were punished

❑ Someone punished us far more than was called for

❑ And so forth – if you don't do what we say, you'll get it

Recall times when you were growing up when you <u>did and did not</u> get punished when you were trying to do something someone wanted you to do. Try to remember how each time felt. Did this happen often?

<u>Write a brief description of what happened, and how it felt:</u>

<u>Does it happen a lot now in your life? Write additional thoughts here:</u>

```
┌─────────────────────────────────────────┐
│                                           │
│          MEDIEVAL TIMES                   │
│                                           │
│              DIRECTIONS                   │
│         ┌────────────────────┐  P        │
│    R    │ • Disease, plagues │  U        │
│    E    │ • Kidnapping       │  N        │
│    W    │ • Barbarism        │  I        │
│    A    │ • Man in control   │  S        │
│    R    │ • Woman/child weak │  H        │
│    D    │ • Goal is "protection" │ M     │
│    S    └────────────────────┘  E        │
│                                  N        │
│                                  T        │
└─────────────────────────────────────────┘
```

If we could only return to the good old days

This three-dimensional method of motivating others has been around forever, and was prevalent during medieval times. This is when <u>feudalism</u> ruled the day, with land barons, lords and priests who dominated small territories in Europe and Asia. These dictators ruled the people, <u>protecting</u> them from:

❑ Diseases and plagues which ran rampant across the land
❑ Other feudal strongholds which were kidnapping women and children/youth
❑ The general barbarism of the times if people did not obey the rules of the land

This basic <u>protectionism</u> assumed: (1) Men are in control, and (2) Women and children/youth are weak.

For Euro-Americans, this <u>feudal model</u> replaced our earlier <u>tribal</u> background. The only tribes remaining at that time were the Gypsies in Europe, who did not want to be ruled by these feudal masters and roamed the countryside in caravans. At that time mankind had yet to meet and conquer the Native American tribes.

For those who lived in feudal times, their quality of life depended entirely on how benevolent their dictators were during good and bad times. So it is today in many homes, classrooms and workplaces -- the quality of life depends on the mood and whims of a dictator (called dad, mom, teacher or boss).

<u>Did [or do] directions, rewards and punishment affect your quality of life? Jot thoughts here:</u>

LIFE IS HUMOROUS

History is full of stories when warlords took over someone's territory and ruled people accordingly. We go to medieval fairs to see and feel what it was like back then. Some kids feel it is like that growing up – like they have "no say". It's funny to watch infants learn to say "mine" or "no" almost as fast as "mama" or "dada".

We live in a world that is truly comical in its ritual to conquer and control others. There are many TV programs where the family, workplace, friendships or military units are fighting among themselves for control and freedom. We laugh at these situations because in a way it makes us feel good that others might have things as bad [or worse] than we do. We actually are able to look at our own misery and laugh when it is happening to someone else.

Nelson L. Noggle, Ph.D.

To add to the humor, someone is always trying to "get on top". Being the "top dog" is clearly a goal many people aspire to, and find it "fun" as long as they are "making progress getting there".

It gradually becomes fun to "gain at someone else's expense" – and find ourselves saying, "They do it to us, so I ought to be able to do it to them". Then we go and party with others to brag about what we accomplished, or complain about what someone did to us – we can actually create a "pity party".

<u>Write any additional thoughts here:</u>

BEHAVIORISM 101

STIMULUS → RESULTING BEHAVIOR → REWARD OR PUNISHMENT

- The simplest model is the method of choice
- Skinner said it was meant for <u>laboratory rats</u>
- We use it because it seems easy and quick
- It works very well with younger children/youth
- Others have refined it -- now it's ***The Box***

This parenting stuff seems easy at first

Many psychologists and educators have studied the relationship between the methods that work for training animals and those used for counseling and educating people. Among them was a man named B. F. Skinner who developed many different models under the "banner" known as:

❑ "BEHAVIOR MODIFICATION".

Skinner wrote in one of his last books that he was alarmed how parents, educators and others were over-using perhaps the simplest of the models known as the:

❑ "STIMULUS-RESPONSE MODEL".

This is where someone is given a stimulus (direction) and is either rewarded or punished based on the appropriateness of the response (behavior). This model tends to work with younger children/youth, or with those who are learning impaired.

Skinner wrote in one of his last books that this low-level model, upon which so much of education and management relies, is ...

"good for training laboratory rats, not people."

Unfortunately, its simplicity is part of its appeal. Since it is also easy to use, it has become our <u>method of choice</u>. Parents, teachers, and managers use it to control the actions of those for whom they are responsible. It is easy, and it works. At least it works in the short term to get one person to do a specific thing. In the long term, its reapplication is necessary each time and for each new expectation; plus the applied consequences must seem fair to everyone involved especially as age and other conditions change. Unfortunately, the responsibility for being motivated often remains with the parent, teacher or boss.

Self-motivation does not flourish under a steady diet of behavior modification.

WHY ARE SO MANY PEOPLE VULNERABLE TO BEING CONTROLLED BY OTHERS?

This was the question that parents, teachers and counselors were bothered about. It was clear that too many youth and young adults are being led astray by their peers with the promise of acceptance along with fun times. It was also clear that they were being led subsequently to alcohol and/or drugs. As I presented this dilemma to a large audience of parents, teachers and counselors, I walked to a corner of the room and meditated and prayed so that I could better help myself and others understand the power of what was going on. It was at that moment that **The Box** was revealed to me – the way in which modern times had taken behavior modification to a brand new level. <u>Make things fun!</u>

Interviews with just about anyone eventually led to the concern about the "work ethic" of youth and young adults. It was as if they were saying:

If it ain't fun, I'm not doing it!

Even interviews with youth and young adults eventually uncovered this startling factor at play in their motivation to do things. And, this was the one thing their peers offered them that the world ruled by adults did not always offer – <u>fun!</u>

It was 1987 when ***The Box*** was revealed to me. It led me to study the implications of what it meant. As I continued to work with parents, teachers, counselors, social workers and business leaders, I soon realized that modern times was fast becoming a test of who can be ruled best and who can do the best ruling. The evidence pointed to the need for greater and greater control, even though the word "empowerment" was being bantered about like some kind of panacea – the world was fast heading toward the following:

***Tell me what to do, tell me what reward am I to get,
how I can avoid punishment, and make it fun!***

Becoming wedded to this only reduces the level of self-motivation to learn something for its own sake. It causes us to learn only as much as is necessary to satisfy the person in charge – to play their game. It also takes away any initiative to do our best, as all we have to do is the minimum necessary to please that person. Pleasing the parent, teacher or boss becomes the main goal – but when we can't please them, we are tempted to turn to someone else – hence children and youth turn to their peers, and young adults work only as hard as is necessary to go off and have a good time.

But, we're advancing our discussion perhaps a little too rapidly. Let's look at how behavior modification has been strengthened to box-in people to do someone's bidding. Let's look at what actually "closes up" The Box to capture and influence someone's motivation. Let's look at the trap we fall into as we dedicate our free will to do satisfy someone else's desire for us. Let's examine it carefully and ask if The Box really causes the kind of motivation that leads to the best learning. For that matter, let's ask if it causes the best motivation for all things asked of us? Or, are we being led into a world of clever enslavement by the sheer manipulation of environmental factors and promised consequences.

<u>Ask yourself – what would you do if you were completely free to do it?</u> <u>Jot thoughts here:</u>

```
┌─────────────────────────────────────────────────────────────┐
│                                                               │
│                   ENTERTAINMENT                               │
│                                                               │
│        DIRECTIONS          ⤳ Someone attempts to motivate     │
│   ┌─────────────────┐        us by making tasks or work fun   │
│ R │               P │      ⤳ Someone promises us a fun        │
│ E │               U │        activity to follow tasks or      │
│ W │               N │        accomplish work                  │
│ A │   The Box      I │      ⤳ Someone makes things fun for    │
│ R │               S │        us after tasks or work is done   │
│ D │               H │      ⤳ Someone ignores us as we do      │
│ S │               M │        our work or tasks in a fun       │
│   │               E │        manner                           │
│   └─────────────────┘ N    ⤳ Someone reinforces fun more     │
│     ┌──────────────┐         than accomplishing hard or       │
│     │ ENTERTAINMENT│         boring work                       │
│     └──────────────┘                                          │
│                                                               │
└─────────────────────────────────────────────────────────────┘
```

Kids seem to respond to having fun

The fourth dimension of *The Box* is called ***ENTERTAINMENT*.** These are the activities or viewpoints our parents, teachers and bosses added to the task or project to help us <u>enjoy</u> whatever it was they told us to do. For example:

- ❏ Someone made the spelling bee fun even if someone failed to spell a word
- ❏ Someone promised us it will be fun if we got through all our spelling words
- ❏ Someone laughed and smiled as we did the things we were told to do
- ❏ Someone ignored that we were horsing around during the spelling bee
- ❏ Someone made it fun rather than having us buckle down and finish our work
- ❏ And so forth – making the activity fun no matter what

Recall times when you were growing up when it <u>was and was not</u> "fun" to do the tasks or projects others asked you to do. Try to remember how each time felt. Did this happen often in the past?

<u>Write down a brief description of what happened in the past, and how it felt:</u>

<u>Does it happen a lot now in your life? Are things you do fun? Jot additional thoughts:</u>

LIFE IS HUMOROUS

"IF IT AIN'T FUN I'M NOT GOING TO DO IT!"

Older people find it fun to visit their grandchild's classroom – and find themselves saying …

> *"Boy they are having a good time in school!"*
> *"It wasn't that way when we're growing up!"*
> *"Having fun wasn't one of the things we*
> *felt about going to school!"*
> *"Kids today really have it lucky!*

Then after reflecting on things in light of what they see happening in today's world, they get a little cynical and begin saying …

Nelson L. Noggle, Ph.D.

> ***"Young people have things too easy!"***
> ***"Young people don't have a good work ethic!"***
> ***"Things can't be fun all the time!"***
> ***"Who is going to get the work done, while everyone is playing?"***

The jokes about the "age gap" are often very funny, yet there is a sad tone to many of them as either the young or the old "take shots at each other".

Write any additional thoughts here:

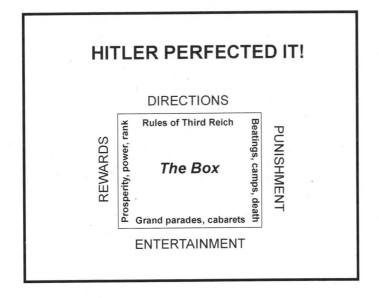

In the 1930's and '40's, Hitler and his henchmen were able to use *The Box* almost to perfection, and succeeded in motivating the German people to commit heinous crimes against other nations and certain people in their own country.

They clearly established a strict climate of rank and order, leading to prosperity and power or internment and death. Hitler was able to *Box-in* an entire nation of people, and almost took over all of Europe in the process. It took the combined power of several nations committed to freedom to overcome the power of Hitler's regime.

Hitler and his propaganda minister knew that people had a basic need to have fun and feel a sense of pride. They made sure the masses enjoyed themselves by taking over the opera, theaters, cabarets and coliseums. They renewed national pride through the pomp and circumstance of grand parades, as well as pubic speeches and patriotic music via the new communication marvel -- the radio. They made it fun for youth and young soldiers to compete, fight and find comradeship together..

This all out abusive use of **_The Box_** turned out to be extremely dangerous, as:

- ❑ The German people were motivated to kill and/or rule other people
- ❑ The German people were made or allowed to feel good while they did it
- ❑ Those who were against it felt frightened and powerless to stop it
- ❑ Desires intrinsic to mankind began to matter less – pleasing Hitler was the goal

Have you ever felt powerless to stop someone in control of you? Jot thoughts here:

LIFE IS HUMOROUS

While war is not funny at all, much of the humor in the world today is made about people fighting wars – as if it is fun to out-maneuver and kill one another. World War II movies, for example, abound with humorous things people did as they prepared to fight battles or celebrated winning them. Many people who fought in wars have commented:

"It was the best time of my life!"

Hitler and his henchmen learned to make ***living in the box*** fun – the Hitler youth became dependent on having fun and getting rewards. The Hitler enemies learned to fear punishment and the loss of wealth, fun and freedom. The German people were programmed to live in ***Hitler's Box***. It is one thing to fight and eventually enjoy "the spoils of war" – but it is quite something else to "have fun while at war".

The Box in its entirety can become "the system" we find ourselves in – and as we see in our various forms of controlling one another, there are those using **The Box** and those finding themselves in it. We see the humor and tragedy of life in all that we do.

Write any additional thoughts here:

DANGEROUS DIMENSION

Adding Entertainment made *The Box* dangerous!

- Hitler was able to "box-in" an entire nation to <u>happily</u> do his bidding
- Unfortunately the growing emphasis in our society is on having fun
- It has become a major part of our reward structure at all levels
- It has become the expectation of work itself -- it should be fun
- It causes parents/teachers headaches, as children/youth expect fun
- It causes managers/supervisors headaches, as workers expect fun
- It causes people to become co-dependent on fun to handle stress
- It causes people to be unhappy if they are not having fun
- Most of all, as we'll show later, it makes youth vulnerable to many of society's ills, such as alcohol, drugs, sexual promiscuity and gangs.

It seems everyone is out to have a good time

When Hitler, as well as rulers both before and after him did, resorted to entertainment to cover up the distasteful aspects of doing his bidding, he was able to establish and maintain psychological control over the German people. He controlled them using all four dimensions of **The Box**. He directed them to do heinous crimes, offered great rewards, threatened and executed horrible punishments, and made life, work and war fun in the Third Reich.

When some parents go about the task of gaining and maintaining total control over children/youth, they run the risk of becoming a dictator, maybe not like Hitler, but none-the-less a dictator. When they do this, they run the risk of stripping children/youth of their own ability to motivate themselves. Soon, pre-teens and teens find themselves boxed-in by the adults in their lives and become susceptible to peer influence, or many other of society's ills.

In the meantime, as these same parents try to maintain control, their work becomes harder and harder. Their own stress levels go up, and they run the risk of resorting to abusive measures or just giving up altogether. It is not too unusual to simultaneously see a youth rebelling from his/her parents and the parents rebelling from the youth.

The Box, which we will show is a useful parenting tool, is like any tool -- when it is used exclusively and/or abusively, it can be dangerous. We start with this reality because so many of today's youth are susceptible to society's ills, and we do not want your child to become one of them. Therefore, we will learn the following:

- ❑ *How to **Use The Box Correctly***
- ❑ *How to **Parent Beyond The Box***
- ❑ *How to **Live Beyond** The Box*

Write any additional thoughts here:

LIFE IS HUMOROUS

Much of the humor we see in society is active "put-down jokes" – having fun at someone else's expense. We learn to do that – we have fun doing it – as long as we are not the targets. Someone asked after seeing a magician's act …

"I wonder how the rabbit feels."

Tucked in this are the many different ethnic jokes we laugh at, with a tongue-in-cheek attitude. Again, we do this at someone else's expense.

Let's be honest – maybe it is fun to see another person suffer, when it isn't us. This is really what many call "sick humor".

It isn't fun to be boxed-in – but it is fun to box others in. Hence, having fun has become the new value system – but feeling we are "in control" is the "true humor" in it all – we delude ourselves into feeling good.

Nelson L. Noggle, Ph.D.

Most people are not malicious in their humor – but they have been "conditioned" to use it and expect it. Unfortunately, it is an extension of a desire to "put someone in their place". The ultimate purpose of **The Box** is to control what others think and do. It has become part of our sense of humor.

<u>Write any additional thoughts here:</u>

The Box TODAY

DIRECTIONS

REWARDS

- Generational model
- Parenting skills
- Education methods
- Management styles

PUNISHMENT

ENTERTAINMENT

If it was good enough for me

it is good enough for my kids

Unfortunately, ***The Box*** is the generational model for most Euro-Americans and drives much of our parenting skills, education methods and management styles -- over the centuries we've lost our tribal roots. The more nurturing ways of allowing competence to mature through *instruction and practice* have been replaced by the accelerated pace of the modern methods of *train and do.*

We've become less cooperative and more competitive, even to the point of:

- ❑ *A lost sense of family*
- ❑ *A lost sense of community*
- ❑ *Growing distrust of government*
- ❑ *More conflict and stress*
- ❑ *Increasing rates of crime and violence*
- ❑ *Greater desire for material gratification*

Had you ever thought of these issues as being the result of too many people trying to boss and change others? Are there too many people trying to use ***The Box*** or trying to get out of it? Jot your thoughts here:

CONSEQUENCES OF *The Box*

LIFE IS HUMOROUS

We find ***The Box*** being used in every aspect of our life. We have emotional feelings about what we have to do to gain rewards, avoid punishment and have a good time. We even have jokes we tell about such feelings …

> ***"I really told off someone on the highway today – I wish I
> had my windows down so he could have heard me?"***

> ***"I've found a way to get my kids to go to school – I tell
> them about the work I need them to do if they stay home –
> and I'm glad they don't take me up on it!"***

> ***"You know, John is just in it for himself – so I offer him a
> hand once in a while so that he doesn't leave me behind!"***

We find ourselves juggling all ***The Boxes*** we find ourselves using to control our situations, and those we find ourselves in. We spend more time looking back over our shoulder being sure ***The Boxes*** are working.

*I'd get ahead faster and better if it weren't for
my co-workers – they need to work on the things
I need them to work on – yeah, right!"*

*"I take three steps forward, and two steps back – only if
feels like I'm always going backward – I want to advance,
but someone is always yelling retreat!"*

<u>Write any additional thoughts here:</u>

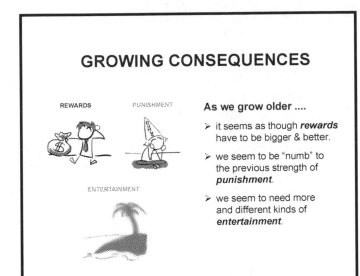

As children/youth grow older, it takes a great deal of time and effort for parents and teachers to come up with **The Box** that is new and strong enough to motivate them. Their growing need for independence fights **The Box,** as other interests and peers become more important to them than going along with "authority figures".

Adults, too, grow numb to ongoing attempts by others to reward, punish and entertain them. The instructors and bosses in their lives represent people they must count on for career and job success, and the financial security they desire. The attitudes and habits adults carry with them out of childhood pertaining to authority figures gives rise to many of the problems they encounter in school or at work. Major problems arise when they encounter instructors or bosses whom overuse or abuse **The Box**, or go too far the other way and fail to provide structure and expectations at all.

Unfortunately, people in a controlled environment grow to expect the treatment they have been getting, and they more often than not want even better treatment. Therefore, managers who use **The Box** will observe more motivation by employees to seek recognition, gain pay raises, and promotions, or escape blame, rather than want to learn how to do a better job.

Have you (or anyone you know) gotten caught up in this continuous cycle of trying to make **The Box** more "just or fair"? Perhaps it was how it was being used on you? Or maybe it was how you used it? <u>Jot your thoughts here:</u>

LIFE IS HUMOROUS

As time goes by, we yearn for tons of money, sunny vacations and big beautiful homes.

We hope for job advancements, fun things to do and fun places to visit.

Getting ahead becomes our "work goal" – having fun and profit become our "pleasure goal" – and traveling becomes our "roaming goal". When we put all these goals together, we "amp up" the consequences of the time we spend – actually beginning to feel the ***Overall Box*** we find ourselves in. We can find ourselves saying …

I can't get ahead at all!"
"If it ain't one thing it's another!"
"Our debt is getting the best of us!"
"My stress is killing me!"
"The more I work, the farther behind we get!"
"Vacations are nice, but the problems are
waiting for me when I get back!"

Nelson L. Noggle, Ph.D.

YOUTH BLAME ADULTS!

➤ Don't know it's *The Box*
➤ Blame parents/teachers
➤ Turn to their peers
➤ Peers use *The Box*
  - Do what we do
  - To be accepted by us
  - So we can have fun
  - Or, you'll be left out
➤ Trade one *Box* for a*nother*

After awhile kids feel boxed-in by adults

Children/youth do not know it's *The Box* -- they think the problems they are having are the <u>adults</u> who are controlling their lives. So, they begin to turn to their peers for understanding and support. Unfortunately, 80% of their peers are a product of *The Box*, and they also use *The Box* to seduce and/or control each other. For example: "You should change your hair style.... that is, if you want to run with us.... wow, now you look better.... let's go party!"

<u>When or if they could wake up to what is happening, they would discover they just traded one *Box* for another. Have you ever witnessed this in other children/youth? Please describe here:</u>

<u>Do you remember this happening to you when you were growing up?</u> <u>Please describe here:</u>

The important thing to remember here is that ***The Box*** may have permeated our lives when we grew up -- it might have been the <u>method of choice</u> by adults and kids alike.

<u>Write any additional thoughts here:</u>

LIFE IS HUMOROUS

Many teenagers feel that adults are trying to keep them from doing what they really want to do. It is hard, almost laughable to them, to see any value to the restrictions and directions adults try to force upon them. Sometimes teenagers wonder if adults know what is going on ...

"Do they have a clue?"

What makes this even more hilarious, yet many times almost tragic, teens often see more sense in what their friends say and do – even if they have been warned by their parents and teachers otherwise. It is as if being accepted by their friends is the most important thing on Earth. It is sad to contemplate, but teens look like they have little or no self-esteem at all ...

"I sure hope they like me!"

Smoking, drinking and partying become the things to do – after all, many adults are doing this and having a ball. Many teens feel ...

"If they say "no" it must be fun!"

Do you remember what it was like being a teen? Were you wishing you could be an adult and do what you wanted to do without the hassle from your parents?

<u>Write any additional thoughts here:</u>

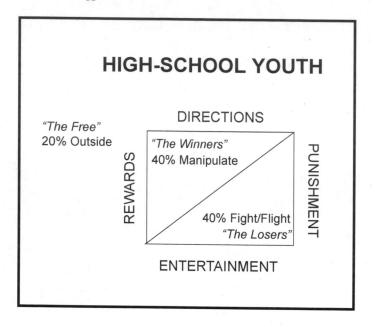

When we look at high-school youth, we see about 40% who are doing quite well and are "winning" in **The Box**, as they manipulate it to get good grades and other rewards, to avoid punishment, and to have a good time. These <u>winners</u> are more interested in winning than learning or succeeding. For example, they want to know what is on the test, will cram the night before, will argue over items they missed, and will forget most of what they committed to short-term memory the night before. They often lack the competence that their grades suggest. Many have exaggerated self-esteem.

Another 40% seem to be "losing" in **The Box**, as they entertain themselves, take whatever punishment they get, and get their rewards from others like themselves. Unfortunately, the winners and authority figures begin to treat these individuals like <u>losers</u>, and they get stuck in the aimless cycle of victimization and lost self-esteem. In many cases, they commit their self-directed learning toward acts of cunning and survival. In today's words -- they become "street smart".

Only about 20% seem to be free of **The Box**, as they seek to improve themselves and their capabilities, worry less about rewards, punishment and entertainment, and help others to succeed, too. They seem to be self-directed learners and workers. Their self-esteem tends to be sturdy, yet realistic given their increased awareness of their capabilities or lack thereof. They tend to hate ***The Box***, but can learn to cope with it.

The 80% caught in ***The Box*** are "at risk"! <u>Describe what you think about this here:</u>

LIFE IS HUMOROUS

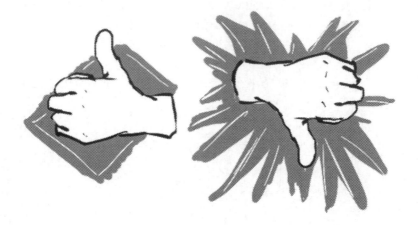

One thing is clear – someone is always looking in to see how we are doing. And, we often wonder what they are thinking ...

"Am I a winner or a loser?"

But, it often doesn't matter what adults say about students, the "winners" and "losers" alike seem far too proud of their designation. They both have learned to cope in *The Box*, healthy or not ...

- ❑ Winners just ask, "What do I need to do to get the rewards?" And they press teachers to make things fun.
- ❑ Losers just ask, "What do I need to do to have fun?" And they try to minimize any punishment they get.

In both cases, the pressure is on the teacher to make things fun ...

"If it ain't fun, I'm not going to do it!"

In both cases, the real risk is that the students are learning to play a game, instead of making learning their goal. Instead, they do crazy things so that they win in ***The Box***". Both feel like winners, each learning the bare minimum to squeak through by pleasing the teacher.

<u>Write any additional thoughts here:</u>

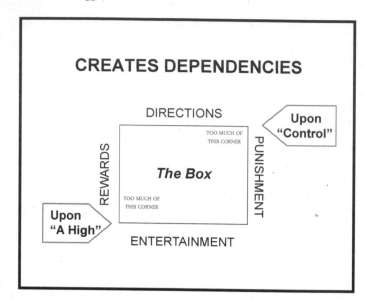

Many say we have become a co-dependent society

A steady diet or an abusive form of ***The Box*** creates one or both of the following:

A Dependency on Control: the need to rely on others even those we fear for direction, rather than to be self-directed and responsible for our own actions. Those given too much or too strong of this corner of ***The Box*** often find themselves later in life with sick relationships in which they are being "ruled" or they are doing the "ruling", such as becoming an abusive or abused spouse, or becoming a gang member or gang leader.

A Dependency on a High: the need for rewards and entertainment and all the good feelings that go along with it. Those given too much or too strong of this corner of ***The Box*** are more susceptible to being seduced or manipulated into parties, alcohol, drugs, sex, or "getting off" on the misery of others.

When either or both of these dependencies are too strong, a person "feels lost" unless their needs are met, and they go looking for people or situations that will fulfill those needs -- they form what is often referred to as:

Co-Dependent Relationships -- when people continue to reinforce the behaviors of others so that they themselves feel safe, protected, good, excited, etc. Example, when the wife of an alcoholic enables the alcoholic to continue drinking rather than take a stand that might threaten the relationship.

Do you know someone who is dependent on *control*, or on *a high?* Describe it here:

LIFE IS HUMOROUS

NEED A HIGH NEED CONTROL

Under too much of **The Box**, we grow dependent upon always motivating us – we grow to lack self-motivation – with four possible examples …

- ❏ Dependency upon **"getting a high"** [to become motivated]
- ❏ Dependency upon **"giving a high"** [to motivate another]
- ❏ Dependency upon **"having control"** [to motivate another]
- ❏ Dependency upon **"being controlled"** [to become motivated]

In any case, we can grow **dependent on The Box** to basically live our lives – people using it on us, and us using it on others. It's as if **The Box Is Life**.

ADULTS BLAME ADULTS!

➢ Don't know it's *The Box*
➢ Feel "victimized"
➢ Blame boss, spouse, co-worker, customer, etc.
➢ Turn to others for help
➢ Others use *The Box*
  ‹ Think like we think
  ‹ We will be your friends
  ‹ So we can have fun
  ‹ Or, you are on your own
➢ Traded one box for another
➢ Remain feeling "victimized"

Victimization can grow faster than maturation

Adults also don't know it's *The Box* -- they think the problems they are having are <u>other adults</u>. So, just like they did as kids, they begin to turn to their peers for understanding and support. Unfortunately, 80% of their peers are a product of *The Box*, and they also use *The Box* to seduce and/or control each other. For example: "You shouldn't let him treat you that way!" "I like people who fight him" "I don't like wimps, especially when it comes to him" "You did it -- you stood up to him -- let's go celebrate!"

<u>When have you felt the need to turn to someone for support, rather than working it out directly with the person or authority figure? Describe it here:</u>

It isn't necessarily bad to turn to others for support -- in fact many people do not do it enough or cannot trust others enough to try it. The key thing here is that it can be problematic to trade one dependency for another. What we probably need to look for is someone to help us become more self-directed, not less -- a sounding board -- not another set of directions, rewards, punishment and entertainment. Don't just turn to another ***Box***.

The problem with "the misery loves company" syndrome is that it perpetuates negative feelings about authority figures or about anyone having power over our destiny. It is easy to get caught up in a cycle of victimization, causing the feeling that "I can't win without losing!"

<u>Write any additional thoughts here:</u>

LIFE IS HUMOROUS

Road rage is an outgrowth of being ***Too Boxed In***, or <u>not</u> being able to successfully ***Box in Others***. There are many signs of our feeling like a victim to other people. Just as kids blame parents and teachers, adults blame teachers, bosses and spouses. It doesn't matter if we are in their box, or are using it ourselves ...

"If it isn't working, it's their fault!

As people get boxed in, or fail at getting others to do what they want, stress sets in ...

Stress
Seems to be
Getting worse
In
Today's world!!!!

Nelson L. Noggle, Ph.D.

VICTIMIZED FEELINGS

- I can't succeed without failing.
- All they see are my mistakes.
- They're all against me.
- What did I ever do to them?
- This is a lose-lose situation.
- It is all a great big set-up!
- They'll get their way as always.
- Nobody seems to understand.
- Does anybody care???

Help!

The power they have over me renders me powerless.

Whose decision is that?

It is only a small step to move from dependent thinking to *victimized feelings*. A person who is "owned" by **The Box**, begins to feel misunderstood, put down, trapped, held back, devalued, and can ultimately be owned by one or more of the following feelings:

- ❑ *Helpless*
- ❑ *Hopeless*
- ❑ *Worthless*

When anyone who routinely feels one or more of these ways, <u>it is time to get help</u>:

One of the strongest and most courageous things a person can do is to reach out for help when things get us down. We are not alone, even when we feel we are.

It is important to reach out in the right direction, such as a professional counselor. We need to rely on someone who has been properly trained and is well experienced in helping people sort out and deal with the complex combinations of past experiences and current situations that box us in.

In the meantime, it is important to remember that ***The Box*** we are in is really nothing more than a strong combination of:

Directions	***Rewards***
Punishment	***Entertainment***

But it often feels like a lot more. It is a logical combination of things that can be sorted out and dealt with in a meaningful way – and that often takes the right kind of help.

<u>Write any additional thoughts here:</u>

LIFE IS HUMOROUS

Victimized people get "stressed out" – they often seek out help from someone to take care of the symptoms of their stress. But some people who grow **dependent upon The Box** often resort to self-medication to **get a high** ...

"LET'S HAVE ANOTHER ROUND OF DRINKS ...

"GIVE ME ANOTHER CUP OF COFFEE ...

"I'M GOING OUT FOR A SMOKE ...

"CAN'T WAIT TO GET HOME AND EAT ...

"WHAT'S ON TV TONIGHT???????

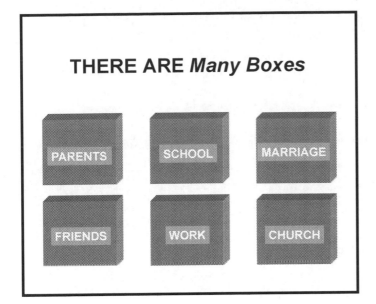

THERE ARE *Many Boxes*

PARENTS SCHOOL MARRIAGE

FRIENDS WORK CHURCH

The Box is an integral part of our society

There are many "*boxes*" that affect our lives:

❑ *Parents* applied **The Box** to teach, guide and discipline us, as we were growing up; and some parents still use it on us even after we grow up.

❑ *School teachers*, counselors and principals applied **The Box** to teach us basic skills, and to prepare us for work, college and life.

❑ *Marriage* is where our spouse and children/youth use ***The Box*** to get us to do things, or to change our ways to please them.

❑ *Friends* also use **The Box** to get us to do things, or to change our ways to please them; they are often a source of peer pressure.

❑ *Work* is where bosses, co-workers (again peer pressure), customers or vendors use **The Box** to get us to do things or change our ways to please them.

❑ *Church* is where ministers, priests, rabbi's (etc.) use **The Box** to get us to do things or change our ways to please them or God.

Nelson L. Noggle, Ph.D.

<u>Are there any other "*boxes*" in your life? Describe them here:</u>

One of the simplest definitions of "mid-life crisis" is when we realize that all we've been doing over the years is trading **Boxes**; and even if we've been winning, we now realize it's not enough -- <u>there is got to be something more to life</u>.

<u>Write any additional thoughts here:</u>

WHEN IS *The Box* BAD?

➤ ***The Box*** isn't bad in and of itself.
➤ Abusive forms of ***The Box*** are bad.
  ▪ Drastic physical or emotional punishment
  ▪ Total lack of rewards and entertainment
➤ A steady diet of ***The Box*** is bad.
  ▪ Too many people using it (too many boxes)
  ▪ Too frequent of a use of it (micro-managing)
➤ Neglect is bad (nobody teaching or guiding)

Some Boxes are safe, others are uncomfortable, and others are abusive.

The Box isn't bad in and of itself. It is not wrong to tell people what we expect of them and what they will get in return for their actions. It is the simple contractual model used in homes, schools, businesses, etc. I am not trying to scare you.

However, when ***The Box*** is <u>abusive</u> physically or emotionally, it tends to create emotional reactions that can ultimately lead to aberrant behavior patterns. The trauma of abuse often causes the victim to seek out other abusive relationships, to abuse their children/youth, or to abuse other weaker members of society. In other words, they look for:

❑ Another ***Abusive Box*** *to* live in, or
❑ A chance to use an ***Abusive Box*** themselves.

A <u>steady diet</u> of ***The Box*** at every turn tends to create strong emotional dependencies and box-like behavior patterns. When parents, teachers and other important adults in a person's life are constantly using ***The Box***, the individual tends to feel totally <u>boxed-in</u>. People suffering from this are extremely susceptible to peer influence, as they:

❑ Trade one ***Box*** for another, and
❑ Use ***The Box*** on one another.

Whether it's abuse or a steady diet, ***The Box*** can dramatically deflate self-esteem, making an individual extremely susceptible to obsessive levels of victimized thinking and such pitfalls as alcohol, drugs, gangs, sexual liaisons, crime, and violence. Their mental, emotional and physical health can literally lie in the balance. Statistics suggest that our society has increasing percentages of people suffering in this way. This is another reason why I decided to write this book.

PREVENT LOW SELF-ESTEEM

WHAT ABOUT NEGLECT?

> ➤ Neglect leads to searching for **The Box**
> ➤ children/youth need boundaries
> ➤ They seek out someone to get them
> ➤ It could be anyone at anytime
> ➤ **The Box** a child finds is often abusive
> ➤ Neglect, therefore, is also abusive

If we dis not need others, we would be on Earth alone.

For some children/youth, parents provide no boundaries at all -- this is <u>neglect</u>. They are allowed to run free with little or no limits on their behavior much of the time.

Children/youth need boundaries -- yes, they need **The Box.** If they don't get it at home, they will seek it out from somewhere else.

The Box a child finds at random may not be a healthy one -- it may be from siblings, peers, or other adults. They experience a lot of inconsistencies -- as teachers look different than the parents and become the enemy. Constant neglect is abusive.

<u>Have you observed or been in situations of heavy neglect? If so describe them:</u>

Children/youth need <u>consistent boundaries</u> that begin to help establish for them the norms that society expects of them, such as:

- ❑ How to treat others and relationships
- ❑ How to fulfill responsibilities as a citizen
- ❑ How to promote physical and mental growth, health and hygiene
- ❑ How to set and follow recreational, educational, career and family goals
- ❑ How feelings about oneself compares with feelings about others

LIFE IS HUMOROUS

As crazy as it sounds, ***The Box*** is important for all of us in order to grasp what people around us expect of us. At an early age, or for someone who is immature, it helps to establish guidelines for behavior – guidelines that outline what happens if we follow them or don't. Tied to ***The Box*** is whether or not a person in it feels like they have a choice. For most things, except things of extreme safety issues, giving a child some sense of choice helps to establish a problem-solving approach to decisions. Heavy commandments and rigid ***Box-like Rules*** often takes the thinking out of the situation – as the child worries more about the rewards/punishment for pleasing us instead of choosing wisely to follow the rule.

NO RULES – NOW WHAT?

NO BOX – NOW WHAT?

NO ENFORCER – NOW WHAT?

The issue actually depends on when we want our children to learn to think for themselves? If they always have us filling their minds with what to do or not to do, they learn to wait for us to decide what they are to do. For the short term, this seems to work – but when they are faced with "rules versus friends", their friends often reset the rules for them and they are easily a pawn to "peer influence".

DO AS I SAY, OR DO WHAT IS BEST?

Ultimately, we want our children to grow up and be able to make wise decisions. Children who are "neglected" have trouble doing that – but so do children who are "over controlled".

Nelson L. Noggle, Ph.D.

Hey, come with us!

What do I do?

<u>Write any additional thoughts here:</u>

SUMMARIZING *The Box*

➢ ***The Box*** is the method of choice by parents and teachers.

➢ It is the unique combination of directions, rewards, punishment and entertainment.

➢ Psychologists refer to forms of it as "behavior modification".

➢ A steady diet of it causes "boxed-in" victimized feelings.

➢ Abusive forms of it causes traumatic victimized feelings.

➢ Neglect or the total absence of it is causes problems, too.

The Box is used to shape children, but into what shape?

The Box is the typical method used by parents today. Yes, even in what we call the permissive era, ***The Box*** prevails. While there is less "corporal punishment" there is more manipulation.

Parents are constantly working to find ways to manipulate children/ youth, while the kids are constantly working to manipulate back. Unfortunately, there are too many abusive parents.

Until just recently, teachers have prescribed to ***The Box*** as a means of establishing classroom control. Under the general banner of "behavior modification", they used various forms of assertive discipline that spelled out consistent consequences for inappropriate and appropriate behavior. Just as with parents, manipulation became the major game plan for teachers and students alike.

The ***"Boxed-in"*** and sometimes traumatized feelings from childhood have led to high levels of victimization among today's youth and young adults. Even many of those who succeeded in ***The Box*** feel victimized by adult authority figures, which tends to complicate their relationships with significant others, bosses and friends.

Nelson L. Noggle, Ph.D.

Do you think there is too much of *The Box* used by parents and teachers today? Why?

Some say we are too lenient today – but maybe today's *Box* is a **CON JOB** -- hence more manipulation than outright force. What do you think?

MICHAEL IN *The Box*

69

Did or does *The Box* impact me?

"TERRIBLE TWO'S"

A two-year old does not wake up one day and decide to be terrible.

<u>What does the phrase "terrible two's" mean to you? Briefly describe here:</u>

When children/youth escape the age of infancy, somewhere between one and two years of age, they begin to assert themselves differently than just crying or wandering around. Their minds now remember things, and they start to actively seek out what they want and run from what they don't want. Many times at this stage of maturity, they lack the language skills to understand many things rationally, so their emotions often rule their behavior.

It is at this stage when parents realize the need for using *The Box* differently than before. Parents begin to feel that they need to *control* this almost limitless energy and boundless exploration, if not for the safety of the children/youth at least for the sanity of the parents themselves. It is at this stage and until about four or five when the parents set in motion their *strategic approach* to parenting.

It is at this stage when parents feel in most need of controlling their children/youth and can get in the habit of using only *The Box*. When this happens, children/youth learn to play the game of complying with or rebelling against the parent rather than learning to think and choose for themselves on the merits of what is before them -- *a **steady diet** of The Box is starting.*

In the pages that follow, let's follow the stages of growth in the case of Michael, who got a steady diet of *The Box*. In his case, people tried to "rule his behavior".

Michael at 3

> ➤ Michael is 3 years old.
> ➤ His parents both work.
> ➤ His grandma baby-sits him.
> ➤ He is a very curious child.
> ➤ He has no siblings.
> ➤ His parents and grandma demand good behavior.
> ➤ They all use **The Box**.

Corralling all that energy is very difficult.

Michael is three years old and is very curious. He gets into everything, and is stubborn. His parents both work, so his grandma baby-sits him every day during the week. When his parents get home, they are tired. So is grandma.

Everyone uses **The Box** with Michael. Expectations are extremely high, so Michael is told what to do and what not to do. He is justly rewarded and punished accordingly. One of the rewards is being allowed to do fun things if his behavior is good.

When his parents get home, things don't usually go so well. Michael acts out and is hard to deal with until after dinner or time for bed. Sometimes bedtime is not good, either. But Michael's parents are consistent, as they reward good behavior and punish bad behavior at all times. And, when things are going well they try to have fun with him.

Grandma has trouble almost every morning after Michael's parents go to work. But by lunch, she has things pretty much under control. She usually can't wait for Michael's naptime. She makes him stay in bed for about an hour and a half, whether he's asleep or not; and sometimes extends it if he's done something bad.

Michael is not a hyper child, but his curiosity can get him into some trouble, especially with his grandma during the day, and with his parents when they first get home from work or at bedtime.

Michael acts frustrated and stubborn when he is punished or told sternly what to do. His parents and grandma do not like him to be stubborn, and see it as a test of wills which they must win. It often doesn't matter what he is being stubborn about.

In general, though, Michael seems to be happy child, as long as he isn't getting punished. <u>Jot thoughts here:</u>

Michael at 6

- ➢ Michael is 6 years old.
- ➢ His parents both work.
- ➢ His grandma baby-sits him.
- ➢ He's in kindergarten.
- ➢ He is a very curious child.
- ➢ He has no siblings.
- ➢ His parents, grandma and new teacher urge good behavior.
- ➢ They all use ***The Box***.

School can be a difficult place for kids.

Michael is now in kindergarten. At first it was fun, but of late he has been getting into trouble with the teacher for not staying on task and bothering other children/youth. The teacher has 24 in the class, which meets every afternoon. Grandma still baby-sits in the mornings.

When told of his acting out in class, Michael's parents punished him by asking Grandma to take TV away from him after school each time the teacher mentioned she had trouble. When Michael wanted then to go outside and play after school, Grandma said no and made him go to his room and play alone. If he was stubborn, she made him go to bed -- she had told his parents that he still needed a nap, because the school only made them put their heads down for 10 minutes in the afternoon. She had tried to get him to nap before school, but that didn't work.

The routine in the evenings remains pretty much the same, but Michael's parents noticed fewer behavior problems when they first got home. He seemed much gladder to see them when they got home. The main problem they had was that when he was stubborn, it was harder to stop than before.

Bedtime was much less of a problem, which his parents attributed to no naps. But mornings were much more of a problem before his parents went to work. They decided that he needed more of their time on weekends. They believe their parenting strategy is working.

Michael still seems fairly happy when he isn't in one of his stubborn moods. Grandma is having the most trouble, which is perceived as Michael taking advantage of her. <u>Jot thoughts here:</u>

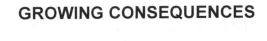

GROWING CONSEQUENCES

REWARDS **PUNISHMENT**

ENTERTAINMENT

As we grow older ....

➤ it seems as though *rewards* have to be bigger & better.

➤ we seem to be "numb" to the previous strength of *punishment*.

➤ we seem to need more and different kinds of *entertainment*.

Well it worked before.

Why not now?

As children/youth grow older, it takes a great deal of time and effort for parents and teachers to come up with **The Box** that is strong and clever enough to motivate them. Their growing need for independence fights **The Box**, as other interests and peers become more important to them than going along with "authority figures".

As Michael grows numb to ongoing attempts by others to reward, punish and entertain him, it takes more insistent directions, bigger rewards, more threatening punishment and fun things that can compete with the fun things he can choose for himself. Parents and teachers can grow weary trying to keep up with "what it takes" to motivate and control Michael. The problem that is brewing is that it is becoming cloudy as to who is the one doing the motivating – as less and less time is spent by Michael to motivate himself.

Unfortunately, people in a controlled environment grow to expect the same treatment they have been getting, and they often want even better treatment. Therefore, parents, teachers and grandma who used **The Box**, saw more motivation by Michael to seek recognition, rewards, good grades, fun times and freedom from blame, rather than to learn how to do well at what he was being directed to do. He began to do only as much as was necessary. Pleasing the one who used **The Box** became the game to be played. Michael was getting good at it.

Do you know of any child [or adult] who is constantly manipulating things to make **The Box** more just or fair? Perhaps you did it yourself growing up, or in a current situation? <u>Jot your thoughts here:</u>

Michael at 9

- Michael is 9 years old.
- His parents both work.
- His grandma baby-sits him.
- He's in the third grade.
- He is a very curious child.
- He has no siblings.
- His parents, grandma and new teacher demand good behavior.
- They all use **The Box**.

Some kids need a firm hand.

Or do they?

Michael is in the third grade, and is getting average grades. His parents think he is doing much less well than he did in first and second grades. His teacher says he shows too little effort and bothers other students when they are working. Michael says he doesn't like his teacher -- "She's mean."

Grandma only baby-sits him when he gets home from school, and when his parents go out in the evenings or on weekends. She says he is much easier to get along with as he watches TV or plays with kids outside. She says that every once in a while she has to punish him for not obeying her or fighting with other kids. She sends him to his room or takes his afternoon snack away from him. He tells his parents, "Grandma gets real mad at me sometimes and yells at me."

Michael's parents have to punish much more severely than before. They feel that his stubbornness is getting out of hand and that he is telling lies to get out of trouble. They view both of these behaviors as terrible, and have dedicated themselves to wiping them out before the holidays. They told Michael that he will get fewer Christmas presents this year if he doesn't act better. His father has had to spank him several times for telling lies.

His teacher tells his parents that they all need to be on the same page because next year in fourth grade schoolwork will get harder and Michael will need better study habits.

Michael has happy times and moody times. When he is stubborn, he is also very angry. He has one friend who he fights with constantly. <u>Jot your thoughts here:</u>

YOUTH BLAME ADULTS!

➤ Don't know it's **The Box**
➤ Blame parents/teachers
➤ Turn to their peers
➤ Peers use **The Box**
  ◦ Do what we do
  ◦ To be accepted by us
  ◦ So we can have fun
  ◦ Or, you'll be left out
➤ Trade one **Box** for a*nother*

After awhile kids feel boxed-in by adults

Even though they learn to manipulate things, and "play the game", children/youth do not know it is ·*The Box* -- they think the problems they are having are due to the <u>adults</u> who are controlling their lives. Even at this early age, Michael turned to Grandma, his peers or the other parent for understanding and support. Unfortunately, most peers are a product of *The Box*, and they also use *The Box* to seduce and/or control each other. For example: "You should change your hair style.... that is, if you want to run with us.... wow, now you look better.... let's go play!"

As for Grandma, or the other parent, "the game" becomes "pitting one against the other". In reality, Michael was just trying to find the "best" *Box*.

<u>He had already begun his life-long habit of "trading one **Box** for another". Have you ever witnessed this in children/youth? Jot thoughts here:</u>

<u>Do you remember "trading **Boxes**" when you were growing up? Jot thoughts here:</u>

The important thing to remember here is that ***The Box*** often permeated our lives as we grew up -- it is the <u>method of choice</u> by most adults and kids alike. <u>Additional thoughts here:</u>

Michael at 15

> Michael is 15 years old.
> His parents both work.
> His grandma baby-sits him.
> He's in the ninth grade.
> He is a very curious youth.
> He has no siblings.
> His parents, grandma and new teachers demand good behavior.
> They all use ***The Box***.

Independence can look like rebellion.

Michael is in the ninth-grade and still gets average grades, except that it's harder for him to keep them at that level. He complains that they don't explain things well enough and that they give unfair tests and stupid homework. His parents have to sit on him to do his homework every night, or he won't do it at all or will do it half-heartedly. They take away privileges like TV, video games, or time with friends if they have trouble with him doing his schoolwork.

Michael is more into friends than his schoolwork, especially his "skater buddies". He and his friends skateboard every day and evening. Sometimes the only time his parents see him is at dinner and when he does homework. His parents have laid down the law about destruction of property, smoking and drugs -- things they've heard that "skaters get into".

Michael's grandma is still there when he first gets home from school, as his parents want to know that he has gotten home. She stays there until one of his parents gets home from work. She occasionally comes over on weekends if his parents go out of town. But she and Michael seldom interact, as he does his thing and she does hers. She told his parents "Don't expect me to make him do his homework."

Michael's teachers feel he doesn't try hard enough, but that he is no trouble in class. One teacher is worried about some of the kids he is running around with because they have had drug problems. When asked by his parents, Michael swears that he has never tried drugs and never will. They believe him, even though they still catch him in little lies about where he is going or where he has been, and are having trouble with him getting home late when he's with friends. Michael doesn't seem happy, especially at home and school, where he thinks everyone bosses him around too much. <u>Jot thoughts here:</u>

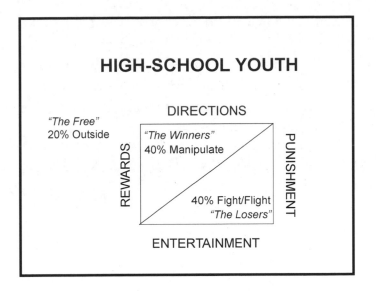

When we look at high-school youth, we see about 40% who are doing quite well and are "winning" in *The Box*, as they manipulate it to get good grades and other rewards, avoid punishment, and have a good time. These <u>winners</u> are more interested in winning than learning or succeeding. Michael fell out of this group -- even learning to "play the game" was not working as well as turning to others for a more favorable *Box*. Michael chose "friends/peers", instead of school, as his priority.

Another 40% seem to be "losing" in *The Box*, as they entertain themselves, take whatever punishment they get, and get their rewards from others like themselves. Michael became part of this group. Unfortunately, the winners and authority figures begin to treat Michael and others like him like <u>losers</u>, and Michael began to get stuck in the aimless cycle of victimization and lost self-esteem. To claim self-esteem, Michael "performed" in ***The Box*** used by his peers, and to some degree used ***The Box*** back on them. He and his skateboard friends actually formed what amounted to be "a new family". Mom, Dad and Grandma had less and less to do with the values Michael was now taking on. Whatever "work ethic", for example, he had was directed toward pleasing his new family.

Only about 20% seem to be free of ***The Box***, as they seek to improve themselves and their capabilities, worry less about rewards, punishment and entertainment, and help others to succeed, too. They seem to be self-directed learners and workers. Michael was a long way from being part of this group – yet, because of his success within his new family; he may have felt like he was freer than before.

<u>Michael was caught up living in ***The Box***—he was "at risk"! What do you think about this?</u>

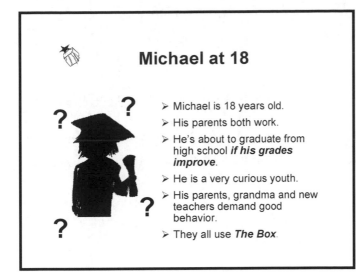

Michael at 18

➤ Michael is 18 years old.
➤ His parents both work.
➤ He's about to graduate from high school *if his grades improve*.
➤ He is a very curious youth.
➤ His parents, grandma and new teachers demand good behavior.
➤ They all use *The Box*.

Uncertain futures come from unsettled pasts.

Michael is in danger of failing his senior year of high school and not graduating. His grades have steadily gotten worse throughout high school, despite his parents making him go to summer school every year. His teachers say he just doesn't try hard, and seems not to care. While he is no particular behavior problem, he is often late to class or cuts classes altogether. Detention only helps for a short period of time.

Michael's parents have been at wit's end trying to get him to do better in school. They think it all started when he was running around with those "skater friends". But when they no longer allowed him to see them, things did not improve.

As one teacher put it, "You have to keep after Michael or he won't do anything -- the only one motivated is the adult trying to get him going." His parents agree; it seems that Michael does not think for himself. He waits for others to dictate what he is supposed to do. The counselor says it is the same way with his friends, "They control what Michael does more than Michael."

Michael is almost always moody, closed off in his room listening to music or playing video games. He almost never has conversations with his mom or grandma. His dad sometimes does something with him on

Saturdays, but they never get into meaningful discussions. Michael told the counselor that "Everyone lectures me; they don't care what I think."

Michael goes out with a bunch of kids every Friday and Saturday night. They stay out too late most of the time, and he sleeps in late afterwards. He had a couple of jobs, but he hated them and quit. He's been seeing a lot of one particular girl lately, but tells his parents nothing about her. He seems oblivious about the danger of not graduating. <u>Jot your thoughts here:</u>

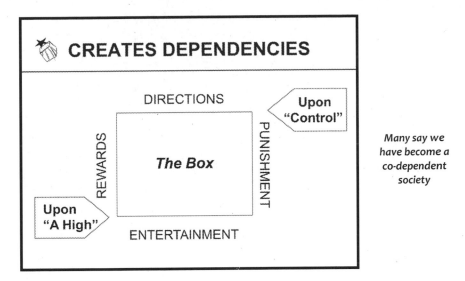

As stated earlier -- a steady diet or an abusive form of *The Box* creates one or both of the following:

A Dependency on Control: the need to rely on others even those we fear for direction, rather than to be self-directed and responsible for our own actions. Michael hated being controlled by his parents, Grandma and teachers. Yet, he was already dependent upon "control", and joined with his skateboard friends where his needs could be met – a better *Box*. Future issues with authority figures and "self-control" were beginning to form.

A Dependency on a High: the need for rewards and entertainment and all the good feelings that go along with it. Michael and his friends had a lot of fun – this where he got away from those who prevented him from enjoying himself. Those given too much or too strong of this corner of *The Box* are more susceptible to being seduced or manipulated into parties, alcohol, drugs, sex, or "getting off" on the misery of others. Perhaps Michael's moodiness suggests he was already into some of this.

When the dependencies are too strong, a person "feels lost" unless their needs are met, and they go looking for people or situations that will fulfill those needs -- they form what is often referred to as:

Co-Dependent Relationships -- when people continue to reinforce the behaviors of others so that they themselves feel safe, protected, good, excited, etc. The skateboard friends were Michael's haven – he needed them and they needed him – feeding upon each other's needs.

<u>Again, do you know someone who is dependent on *control, a high or both?* Jot thoughts here:</u>

Michael at 20

- ➤ Michael is 20 years old.
- ➤ He has limited schooling.
- ➤ He needs a job.
- ➤ His parents both work.
- ➤ He is a very worried person.
- ➤ He runs with his drinking buddies.
- ➤ His parents, grandma and potential employers demand good behavior.
- ➤ They all use ***The Box***.

If I can't have fun at work, I'll find it elsewhere, especially if fun is my goal.

Michael got his GED. His parents made him enroll in a special program that worked toward the GED and prepared him for the world of work. It only took him nine months to get the GED and graduate from the program.

The girl he has been seeing lately is pregnant. She hasn't decided if she is going to get an abortion or not. Michael is more worried he'll have to marry her than having to provide for a child. He says, "I don't believe the kid is mine, anyway."

Michael has had three jobs. He quit one and got fired from the other two. He blames his boss on two of the situations, and the company in the third. He said, "They don't know a good worker when they see one."

He still runs with pretty much the same bunch of friends he did at the end of high school. They go to bars and drink a lot. That's how he met the current girlfriend.

He tells his parents that they should have made him do better in school and should have treated him nicer. He says that his teachers, especially in high school, were awful and that he didn't learn anything that is useful now. They have asked him to go back to the counselor they sent him to during high school -- he won't go, and says, "He will just tell me what to do just like everyone else."

Michael acts very happy go lucky when you see him with friends. But around family or alone, he looks withdrawn and unhappy. He never talks to family about what's going on in his life -- he does talk with one of his drinking buddies.

He doesn't even have money to keep gas and oil in his car; he is constantly having car trouble and counts on one of his buddies for fixing it. Jot your thoughts here:

ADULTS BLAME ADULTS!

- ➢ Don't know it's ***The Box***
- ➢ Feel "victimized"
- ➢ Blame boss, spouse, co-worker, customer, etc.
- ➢ Turn to others for help
- ➢ Others use ***The Box***
  - ◦ Think like we think
  - ◦ We will be your friends
  - ◦ So we can have fun
  - ◦ Or, you are on your own
- ➢ Traded one box for another
- ➢ Remain feeling "victimized"

Victimization can grow faster than maturation

Adults also, don't know it's ***The Box*** -- they think the problems they are having come from <u>other adults</u>. So, just like they did as kids, they begin to turn to their peers for understanding and support. Unfortunately, most of their peers are a product of ***The Box***, and they also use ***The Box*** to seduce and/or control each other. Michael couldn't transfer relationships into his job settings, so it was people he had fun with outside of work that he turned to for support <u>and fun</u>. Drinking has become a big part of Michael's "support mechanism" – in a sense he is self-medicated to relieve himself of the stress he feels. He could easily turn extensively to alcohol or other drugs and not even need other people for support.

It isn't necessarily bad to turn to others for support -- in fact many people do not do it enough or cannot trust others enough to try it. The key thing here is that it can be problematic to trade one dependency for another. Michael had used his peer group for support for a long time – he was so wrapped up in them and what they do that he could not see that it "wasn't working".

The problem with "the misery loves company" syndrome is that it perpetuates negative feelings about authority figures or about anyone having power over our destiny. It is easy to get caught up in a cycle of victimization, causing a feeling, "I can't win without losing!" Adding alcohol or drugs only makes the problem more complex, because under their influence "all seems well".

Again, have you felt the need to turn to someone, drinking or drugs for support, rather than working it out directly with the people and issues involved? Or, has anyone close to you gotten into this kind of cyclical dependency process? Jot your thoughts here:

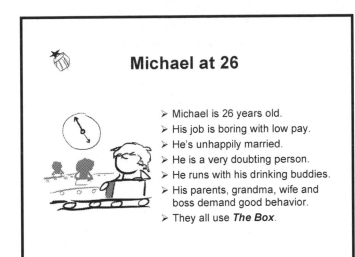

Michael at 26

➤ Michael is 26 years old.
➤ His job is boring with low pay.
➤ He's unhappily married.
➤ He is a very doubting person.
➤ He runs with his drinking buddies.
➤ His parents, grandma, wife and boss demand good behavior.
➤ They all use *The Box*.

Life can become a waiting game.

For what?

Michael was forced to marry the girl he got pregnant. His dad got him a steady job assembling wood cartons. It doesn't pay much, but with what his wife makes they can pay rent, utilities, car payments and credit card debts. They still go drinking a lot with their friends.

Michael is very disgruntled with his job and his boss. But he cannot leave because of the money. His wife wants him to enroll in night classes, but he says he's too tired from his job.

He only gets together with his parents for holidays. They occasionally baby-sit the kids; they have two, now. His parents always ask how he's doing and urge him to go to school or get a better job. He just changes the subject or leaves the room "when they get on that kick".

Except for his friends, whom he believes are "true blue", Michael has real doubts about himself and the future. His wife tells him that he is lazy and that she sometimes wonders why she married him. She scolds him for drinking too much, and tears down his friends. She goes out less often with him to the bars with his friends, both because they can't afford baby-sitters and she doesn't enjoy herself.

Michael is only happy when he is with friends, and that can go away if he drinks too much. He spends little time with his children, and his wife is happy in a way about that because he yells at them too much.

<u>Michael doesn't think about the future -- he just lives day-to-day. Jot your thoughts here:</u>

Where is Michael headed?

VICTIMIZED FEELINGS

Help!

> I can't succeed without failing.
> All they see are my mistakes.
> They're all against me.
> What did I ever do to them?
> This is a lose-lose situation.
> It is all a great big set-up!
> They'll get their way as always.
> Nobody seems to understand.
> Does anybody care???

The power they have over me renders me powerless.

Whose decision is that?

As established earlier, it is only a small step to move from <u>dependent thinking</u> to <u>victimized feelings</u>. A person who is "owned" by *The Box*, begins to feel misunderstood, put down, trapped, held back, devalued, and ultimately one or more of the following:

- ❑ *Helpless*
- ❑ *Hopeless*
- ❑ *Worthless*

When we, or anyone we know, feel this way, it is time to get help:

One of the strongest and most courageous things a person can do is to reach out for help when things get us down. We are not alone, even when we feel we are.

Michael was not able to turn to some healthy enough to pull him out of the cycle of victimization he was living. Because his marriage was a forced thing, he could not turn to his wife for help – and it was likely that she might not be healthy enough to help. Many couples run into added problems when they try to help one another when they are caught living in *The Box*.

In the meantime, it is important to remember that ***The Box*** we are in is nothing more than a strong combination of:

    Directions   ***Rewards***
    Punishment   ***Entertainment***

But it often feels like a lot more. It is a logical combination of things that can be sorted out and dealt with in a meaningful way. This is where professional help is needed. <u>Jot thoughts here:</u>

Michael at 40

> ➤ Michael is 40 years old.
> ➤ He can't get ahead in his job.
> ➤ His marriage is in trouble.
> ➤ His parents are retired.
> ➤ His grandma is in a nursing home.
> ➤ He is a very cynical person.
> ➤ His parents, grandma and boss demand good behavior.
> ➤ They all use **The Box**.

A cynic is someone who goes to others to fight his fights.

Michael has never been able to turn things around. He never went back to school. He just did his job well enough to keep it and become a senior assembler. He requested management positions, but was turned down every time. When he got disgruntled and went to the union representative for help, he was told that his work record and cynical attitude was getting in the way. He has never gotten up the courage to look for another job, even though his wife constantly hounded him to do so.

His marriage is on the rocks. The kids are 12 and 14 years old, and his wife feels they can handle a divorce. She has met another man who owns and runs a thriving business, and she is ready to move on to better things. Michael is caught up in the unfairness of her running around on him, and is blaming her for all his problems. He says that he'd have gotten those management jobs if she had been a more supportive wife. He also blames her for the problems the 12-year old is having.

Michael quit drinking with his buddies; "They kind of moved on and forgot who their friends were." He became a "couch potato", with his head buried in the TV and his six-pack of beer. He and his wife haven't had a meaningful discussion for years. Of course, "That's her fault."

Michael's parents have given up on Michael. They spend more time with the grand- children than they do with him, which is primarily on holidays and birthdays. They have reached the conclusion that Michael was born to be this way.

Michael is bitter, cynical and has begun to feel helpless and hopeless. His wife says, "He is worthless." <u>Jot your thoughts here:</u>

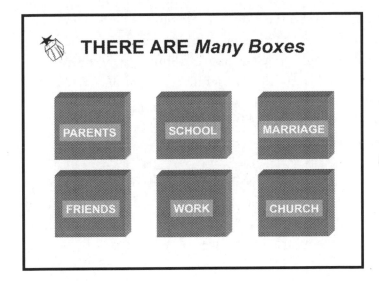

THERE ARE *Many Boxes*

PARENTS · SCHOOL · MARRIAGE

FRIENDS · WORK · CHURCH

The Box is an integral part of our society

Again, there are many ***Boxes*** that affect our lives, and many ***Boxes*** within each kind::

Parents applied ***The Box*** to teach, guide and discipline us, as we were growing up; and some parents still use it on us even after we grow up.

School teachers, counselors and principals applied ***The Box*** to teach us basic skills, and to prepare us for work, college and life.

Marriage is where our spouse and children/youth use ***The Box*** to get us to do things, or to change our ways to please them.

Friends also use ***The Box*** to get us to do things, or to change our ways to please them; they are often a source of peer pressure.

Work is where bosses, co-workers (again peer pressure), customers or vendors use ***The Box*** to get us to do things or change our ways to please them.

Church is where ministers, priests, rabbi's (etc.) use ***The Box*** to get us to do things or change our ways to please them or God.

Michael had trouble with ***The Box*** in nearly all of these cases – and he added the enslavement that heavy drinking causes – as the booze owned him, even though he felt it didn't. Ultimately, he drove away those he thought were just trying to boss him around and/or were trying to manipulate him. He didn't know that he was in effect doing those things to himself. As was said earlier, when we feel helpless, hopeless and/or worthless, we need help!

One of the simplest definitions of "mid-life crisis" is when we realize that all we've been doing over the years is trading ***Boxes***; and even if we've been winning, we now realize it's not enough -- there is got to be something more to life. Jot thoughts here:

WHEN IS *The Box* BAD?

➢ ***The Box*** isn't bad in and of itself.
➢ Abusive forms of ***The Box*** are bad.
  - Drastic physical or emotional punishment
  - Total lack of rewards and entertainment
➢ A steady diet of ***The Box*** is bad.
  - Too many people using it (too many boxes)
  - Too frequent of a use of it (micro-managing)
➢ Neglect is bad (nobody teaching or guiding)

Some Boxes are safe, others are uncomfortable, and others are abusive.

Recall that we said ***The Box*** isn't bad in and of itself. It is not wrong to tell people what we expect of them and what they will get in return for their actions. It is the simple contractual model used in homes, schools, businesses, etc. I am not trying to scare you.

However, when ***The Box*** is <u>abusive</u> physically or emotionally, it tends to create emotional reactions that can ultimately lead to aberrant behavior patterns. The trauma of abuse often causes the victim to seek out other abusive relationships, to abuse their children/youth, or to abuse other weaker members of society. In other words, they look for one or both of these:

❑ Find another ***Abusive Box*** to live in
❑ Start to use an ***Abusive Box*** on others

A <u>steady diet</u> of ***The Box*** at every turn is abusive, too – it tends to create strong emotional dependencies and box-like behavior patterns. When parents, teachers and other important adults in a person's life are constantly using ***The Box***, the individual tends to feel totally <u>boxed-in</u>. People suffering from this are extremely susceptible to peer influence, as they:

❑ Trade one *Box* for another, [Michael turned to his peers] and/or
❑ Use *The Box* on others
❑ Use *The Box* on one's self [Michael eventually boxed himself in with drinking]

Yes, we need boundaries. *The Box* is a reality of our modern society, and the fact that there are so many and so many varieties in a fast-changing world only makes things complex. Can we ever *cope in The Box,* or *live beyond The Box*? <u>Jot additional thoughts here:</u>

SUMMARIZING *The Box*

- ➢ ***The Box*** is the method of choice by parents and teachers.
- ➢ It is the unique combination of directions, rewards, punishment and entertainment.
- ➢ Psychologists refer to forms of it as "behavior modification".
- ➢ A steady diet of it causes "boxed-in" victimized feelings.
- ➢ Abusive forms of it causes traumatic victimized feelings.
- ➢ Neglect or the total absence of it is causes problems, too.

The Box is used to shape children, but into what shape?

The Box is the typical method used by parents and teachers today. Yes, even in what we call the permissive era, ***The Box*** prevails. While there is less "corporal punishment" there is more manipulation. Parents are constantly working to find ways to manipulate children/youth, while the kids are constantly working to manipulate back. Unfortunately, there are too many abusive parents. While Michael was not "abused" physically, some might say he was abused emotionally, as his views constantly had to take a back seat and he had to search for a better ***Box***. When his bosses and wife used ***The Box*** on him, and his friends were not enough support, his drinking became <u>his way out</u> – but it really only sunk him in even deeper.

The "boxed-in" and sometimes traumatized feelings from childhood have led to high levels of victimization among today's youth and young adults. Even many of those who succeeded in ***The Box*** feel victimized by adult authority figures, which tends to complicate their relationships with significant others, bosses and friends. Even jobs, marriages and friendships seem to contain ***The Box*** as a major way to "contract", "If you do that, I'll do this." Even ***Winning in The Box*** can backfire, as we still grow dependent upon "playing the game". If facts were known, some of Michael's friends might have "won" in ***The Box***, but still have felt like they weren't "free". As we said earlier, much of "mid-life crisis" comes from winning in all ***The Boxes***, but being left with the feeling of "so what".

<u>Do you think there is too much of ***The Box*** being used by parents, teachers, bosses and friends today? Even spouses! What else is there? How could life be any different? Jot your thoughts, including why?</u>

GETTING BEYOND *The Box*

Learning to use more than *The Box*

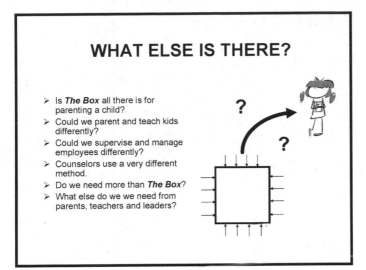

WHAT ELSE IS THERE?

➢ Is **The Box** all there is for parenting a child?
➢ Could we parent and teach kids differently?
➢ Could we supervise and manage employees differently?
➢ Counselors use a very different method.
➢ Do we need more than **The Box**?
➢ What else do we we need from parents, teachers and leaders?

Is it safe to go outside The Box?

Is ***The Box*** the only method for parents, teachers and leaders? How else could we teach and manage others?

Why is it so difficult to break free of ***The Box*** as our primary teaching or leadership method?

Our simple starting point is to remember two things as we proceed from here:

1. Our goal is to help children, youth and adults have more self-control.
2. Our method will be to use less and less of ***The Box***, but use it correctly when we do.
3. And, use ***The Box*** for the right reasons.

A NEED TO *Control*

PROPER CONTROL

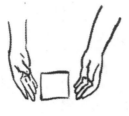

It's Like Being In Good Hands

➢ **The Box** is still an important tool for parenting and teaching.

➢ **The Box** needs to be supportive rather than demanding.

➢ We should control to protect, not to treat people like pawns.

➢ We should provide a **Safe Box** for children, youth and adults in a consistent manner.

➢ We need to use each dimension of **The Box** correctly when we do use it.

Control needs to look safe, and be safe!

There is no mistake about it -- **The Box** is a vital tool for teaching and managing children, youth and adults. The main goal of control provided by **The Box** should be to protect the person from doing something that is not in their best interest, especially if they lack the maturity to make such a choice wisely, don't have the interest to do it at all, or don't have the knowledge and skills to give it a good try. But, it is not to be used to "rule" or "possess" someone Think back to times when you used **The Box** well -- why did it go well?

If you cannot remember when you used **The Box** well, maybe you can remember when it was used well on you -- why did it work so well?

A NEED TO *Nurture*, TOO

➢ Trust -- the learner needs to be in an environment which freely and safely lets them to learn from their own efforts.

➢ **Relevance** -- the learner needs to see that the things to be learned or done are important to them now or in the future.

➢ **Balance** -- less and less control is needed as the learner's self control and self motivation grows and matures.

Like Learning to Ride a Bike

Nurturing begins by using The Box wisely; then knowing when and how to go beyond it.

It's like learning how to ride a bike. When the child watches other children riding bikes, and thinks about where they can go and how fast they can get there on a bike, he/she begins to have an inner desire to ride a bike, too. This initial motivation has to be both nurtured and controlled. Parents need to encourage, guide, teach and at the same time protect their child as he/she learns to ride. Teachers and leaders of youth and adults need to both nurture and control, too.

Parents put on "training wheels" to reduce the chances of falling and to speed up the learning time. By doing this, it reduces the chance for negative motivation to take over, such as fear of being hurt or that it is too hard to learn. The parent also walks along side of the child for the first few attempts to lend support at least until "he/she starts to get the hang of it". Then the child develops more skill, and eventually the parent stands away and watches as the <u>child rides by itself</u>. At some point the parents go inside while their child rides outside with the training wheels. Then, as the child's skill level and confidence increase, the parents raise and eventually remove the training wheels. Less and less control is needed, as they get better.

<u>Explain what you believe is the role of both nurture and control in this bike example:</u>

AS PEOPLE MATURE

Expand and relax *The Box* :

➢ Avoid simply strengthening *The Box*

➢ Allow them to set own boundaries

➢ Move more to natural consequences

➢ Teach them how to recognize *The Box*

➢ Teach them how to avoid *Unhealthy Boxes*

➢ Free them to become more self-motivated

More freedom is nature's reward for maturing.

Avoid simply strengthening The Box. One of the temptations facing parents, teachers and leaders is that people under their care may expect *The Box*, and that is needed is to increase the size of the rewards, to increase the severity of punishment, and to change the age-level appropriateness of entertainment.

Allow people to set their own boundaries. Early uses of *The Box* cause people to expect it as our primary method of parenting, teaching or managing. One way to "wean" them from needing to be controlled, is to involve them in setting boundaries, including all four dimensions of *The Box*.

Move more to natural consequences. When they are setting boundaries for themselves, discuss what the likely outcomes would be if they do or don't succeed as desired. When the outcome actually occurs (any level of success or non-success), become more willing to let the natural consequence of the action prevail.

Teach people how to recognize The Box. It becomes important for yourself as well as the one under your care to recognize when someone is using *The Box* to get you [or them] to do something. Ultimately, people need to be able to understand their choices so that they do not totally give their freedom to choose to someone else. It is one thing to be "directed" or "supervised", but it is quite another thing altogether to be "possessed", "ruled" or "owned".

Teach people how to avoid unhealthy boxes. It is possible for some people to use *The Box* on those under your care for their own purposes, be it pressure to dress or behave in an inappropriate manner, do things their way, try drugs or alcohol, experiment with their sexuality, or commit acts of crime or violence. People need to have an inner strength that is greater than *The Box* that is used on them.

<u>Write any additional thoughts here:</u>

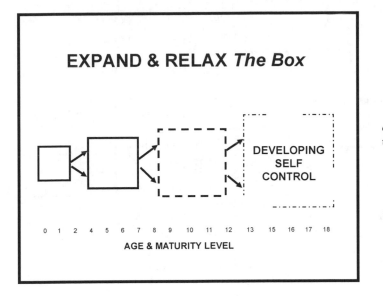

As children, youth and adults mature, we need to expand and relax **The Box**. The goal is to help the person develop more self-control and self-motivation.

Please list the major "must have" capabilities you think youth need to have by the time they are 18 (or when they leave home to live on their own):

Now, looking back on your own upbringing, at what age were you given the opportunity to truly practice those kinds of capabilities? How often did you feel as you were growing up that you were being forced to wait for life to begin after you left home? Why does this happen?

There is a "generational" nature to **The Box**. We often do what our parents did.

NOT JUST *The Box*

PREVENT A "STEADY DIET" OF *The Box*

➤ Delegate more responsibility
➤ Free them to learn from own success or failure
➤ Give fewer detailed directions
➤ Allow more shared decision making
➤ Parents, teachers and leaders <u>must</u> provide:
  · *Trusting environment*
  · *Personal relevance*

Subtle forms of abuse stem from over-control

Often over-protection.

Obviously, ***we must avoid using an Abusive Box*** -- there is no good excuse for physical or emotional abuse -- not even our own stress level. ***Never abuse children!***

Preventing a steady diet of The Box is another matter. Due to the generational nature of *The Box* and the reinforcement of behavioral modification as parenting and teaching methods, all of us are "set-up" to use *The Box* on children/youth, not to mention other adults. Three keys to successful parenting, teaching and managing are as follows:

❑ Don't do away with ***The Box*** altogether.
❑ Use it more with forethought and less as a habit or stress reaction.
❑ Depend on it less and less over time.

Here are <u>some goals</u> for preventing a steady diet of ***The Box***:

❑ *Delegated responsibility.* Turn more and more of life over to child as they mature.
❑ *Freedom to learn from success or failure.* Let natural consequences teach.

❑ *More shared decision-making.* Involve them in setting "family" boundaries.
❑ *Key parents, teachers and managers must provide:*

- *Trusting environment.* Provide place to talk, listen and be listened to openly.
- *Personal relevance.* Deal with it in terms of the child's needs and concerns.

<u>Highlight or circle the ones above you need to do more of, and if you are reading this book </u>along with someone else, discuss what you are doing.

How well do you think you avoid using a steady diet of ***The Box****?*

<u>Write any additional thoughts here:</u>

WHAT COUNSELORS DO

To avoid the inquisition ....
To avoid demands ....

Counselors establish ....

☺ a **trusting environment** for the client, which is maintained at all times.

☺ **personal relevance** to the client, which is pursued at all times.

☺ **either one** at any given time, which helps cause and maintain the other.

Why do counselors succeed with our kid, when we don't?

Counselors often succeed where parents, teachers or leaders sometimes cannot. The reason for this is because counselors know that:

- ❏ By providing a *trusting environment*, the person will feel safe and free to discuss and deal with what is important to them -- trust leads to relevance.
- ❏ By dealing with what is *personally relevant*, the person will feel that what is important to them is important to the counselor -- relevance leads to trust.
- ❏ It doesn't matter which is established first, trust or relevance; one tends to lead to the other to stimulate and *nurture* understanding and growth.

What is gained if a person goes to someone and feels safe enough to freely talk about whatever is going on in his or her life?

What's gained for the person?

What's gained for the counselor?

What's gained for the person's relationship with the counselor?

How does a person's friends or peers provide this, (which can be both good and bad)?

Why can't we establish *trust and relevance* instead of ***The Box*** as our method?

Write any additional thoughts here:

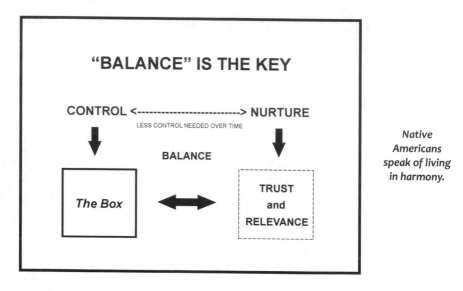

The Box is used most often when we want <u>control</u> over the things that people under our care think, learn and do. But, a steady diet is not necessary.

Maturation is the process by which our children, youth and adults become increasingly more self-directed and responsible for their own choices and actions. <u>Less control and more nurture</u> is what tends to free people to act more independently, without having to rebel against or comply with *The Box*. The maturation process is nurtured, not controlled. Remember, the goal is to nurture self-motivated people.

<u>What are some ways to nurture the emotional and mental growth of children and youth? List ideas you have thought of:</u>

<u>When done, **categorize** each of your ideas above as **T** or **R**, labeling each as one of the following:</u>

    [T] **TRUST** -- setting a <u>trusting environment</u>
    [R] **RELEVANCE** – focusing on <u>personal relevance</u>

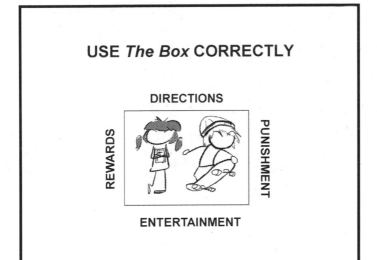

Parenting Beyond The Box, one of the guidebooks, is being designed to more deeply help us **use *The Box* correctly** when we use it. It will prevent us as parents from being too demanding or over-controlling of the children, youth and adults under our care. It will also prevent us from neglecting them and failing to provide enough boundaries. And, it will protect us from abusing them.

It will outline the purpose, strategies and examples for us to draw on as we use each dimension of ***The Box****.* It also will allow us to evaluate how well we are using it at this time.

<u>As you think about using ***The Box*** in the future, list some things here that you already feel you want to accomplish:</u>

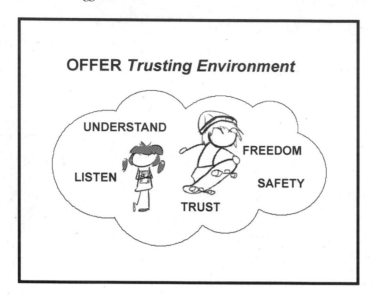

Parenting Beyond The Box Guidebook is designed also to more deeply help us set and maintain a trusting environment within which our children/youth can think, speak and act for themselves so that they can have more self-control over their own lives. The more self-control our children and youth have, the less we have to run their lives for them.

Nurturing our children and youth cannot happen without trust. When they begin to fear us too much or think we don't care about them or believe everything has to be our way, children and youth begin to lower their respect for us and begin to display open rebellion or passive manipulation to get their way. A trusting environment needs to allow them to gradually make more choices and decisions on their own as they grow older, otherwise they cannot mature.

<u>Describe the trust level between you and your parents while you were growing up:</u>

<u>Why do you think having a high trust level is important?</u>

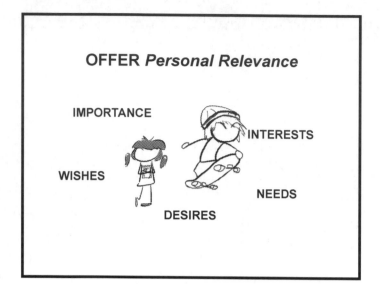

Parenting Beyond The Box Guidebook is designed also to more deeply help us set and maintain relevance for children and youth, such that they see the importance of things they are to do and learn. All of us know that it is much easier to learn or do something if we are interested in it, need it or want to do it. So it is with the children and youth under our care.

Nurturing our children and youth cannot happen without relevance. We as parents need to help our children and youth understand the value of what we expect them to learn and do; teachers in schools need to do the same thing. Many times we as parents need to make up for what teachers fail to do in this area. If we don't **The Box** forces our children and youth to get grades, avoid punishment and wish for more fun and less boredom, instead of learning and doing for reasons that in and of themselves are important.

Describe the things you were interested in or motivated to do growing up, aside from pleasing someone using **The Box**:

If you have children or teens of your own, what are they interested in or motivated to do?

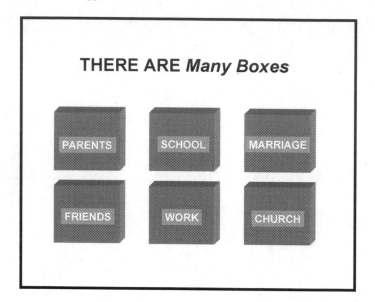

THERE ARE *Many Boxes*

PARENTS   SCHOOL   MARRIAGE

FRIENDS   WORK   CHURCH

The Box is an integral part of our society

Let's be clear about this – **The Box** is used by parents, teachers, friends, husbands, wives, supervisors, managers and church leaders. It is a generational model for motivating people to learn what we want them to learn, to do things, as we want them to do them, and to do so happily and without too much complaining and resistance.

We have been taught and led by people who used **The Box** to get us to do what they wanted. It is as though we entered into a "contract" to do as they directed so that we get something in return, avoid negative consequences and have fun along the way if possible. We live with many of these **Box-like** contracts going on simultaneously – it is "a way of life".

Some of those **Boxes** occurred mostly in the past, while others still affect us directly today. Then there are those from the past that linger in our minds and cause us concerns as we try to live our lives. Some of us have what is referred to as "psychological issues" from the past, either because someone used **The Box** too often, too rigidly or abusively.

On top of that, we ourselves use **The Box** to get others to do our bidding. As parents we try to get our children or youth to do what we want. As teachers we try to get them to learn. As husbands or wives we try to get our spouse to go along with what we want. As friends we try to get others to do things or think the way we do. And as leaders on the job, in clubs or at church we use it to motivate others to do their part.

So, it's ***The Box being used on us and by us*** – and people would say, "So what's new?"

<u>Are you in a cycle of using and being used by **The Box**? Explain:</u>

BECKY BEYOND *The Box*

GOING BYOND *The Box*

- ➤ Michael was raised primarily in *The Box*
- ➤ *The Box* made him into a "victim"
- ➤ Becky, however, was raised differently
- ➤ Her parents raised her *Beyond The Box*
- ➤ Things turned out differently for her

How does going beyond The Box work?

Let's compare Becky with Michael.

As we saw, Michael was raised primarily in *The Box.* His parents, grandmother and teachers used and soon had to use *The Box* to motivate him at all. As her turned to his peers, they too used *The Box* to manipulate him into trying things they did, eventually running him into alcohol and drugs. He had a lot of trouble getting through high school, eventually having to get a GED, and had many difficulties holding onto a job. He had troubles on the marriage front as well. He felt like and acted like a victimized person right into "middle age". He was still in *The Box – many boxes.*

Becky, however, is an example of someone raised *beyond The Box.* As you will see in the following pages, her life turned out very differently than Michael's. Her self-esteem was strengthened by her early life, right into her adult life. She did not feel like a victim, even though she encountered ups and downs like anyone. She progressed through early adulthood and into middle age happily and productively. She could *cope in The Box, avoid unhealthy Boxes and avoid using The Box on others.*

As you follow Becky's story, we will compare it to Michael's along the way. <u>Think of yourself growing up, or a close friend or sibling who grew up when you did. Think of your children, if you are or have been a parent. How much was *The Box* prevalent in failures and successes in your life? Please describe and explain:</u>

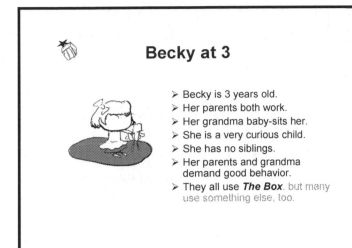

Becky at 3

- ➤ Becky is 3 years old.
- ➤ Her parents both work.
- ➤ Her grandma baby-sits her.
- ➤ She is a very curious child.
- ➤ She has no siblings.
- ➤ Her parents and grandma demand good behavior.
- ➤ They all use ***The Box***, but many use something else, too.

Setting firm but loving boundaries is important at young ages.

Becky is three years old and is very curious. She gets into everything, and is stubborn. Her parents both work, so her grandma baby-sits her every day during the week. When her parents get home, they are tired.

Everyone uses ***The Box*** with Becky at this early age. Expectations are extremely high, but Becky is told what to do and what not to do with encouragement. She is justly rewarded and punished, and encouraged to continue trying.

When her parents get home, things usually go so well. Becky is glad to see her parents and goes on about her business through dinner and time for bed. Bedtime is always good, even if Becky did something wrong earlier. But Becky's parents are consistent, as they reward good behavior and punish bad behavior at all times combined with encouragement.

Grandma has no trouble after Becky's parents go to work. She and Becky look forward to doing things together. She has Becky take a nap every afternoon, and lets her sleep as much as she needs. She never uses naptime as a punishment.

Becky is not a hyper child, but her curiosity can get her into some trouble. Even if her grandma and parents are tired or stressed out, they are careful to avoid overreacting when this occurs.

If Becky acts frustrated or stubborn when she is punished or told what to do, everyone uses a tone of encouragement while still requiring it to be done. Her parents and grandma do not like her to be stubborn, and see it as a sign of independence, which must be guided. They are careful to listen to her and allow her to negotiate when appropriate. In general, Becky seems to be happy child.

<u>Write any additional thoughts here:</u>

🎁 Michael versus Becky at 3

Sometimes pulling is better than pushing a child.

Michael was controlled and taught from the very beginning to, "Do as I say!" It was as though his parents and grandma were determined to "push" him to "do right".

Becky was encouraged more often, yet early on was raised in ***The Box*** as well. Very young children need boundaries, but they also need time and space to think, not just react to ***The Box***. Becky started off being allowed to be more of her own person, than was Michael – hence, Michael started early on to ***fight The Box*** in order to maintain some feeling of independence.

There is a fine line between over-controlling children and providing safe, secure boundaries. But there is a huge gap between over-controlling and spoiling them. This is the time when love and trust from parents begin to show forth – whereas always needing to "control" often squashes them from showing. Remember, children are extremely observant – they see and analyzed every move a parent makes. Rigidly using and wielding a steady diet or abusive forms of *The Box* severely hampers a child's view of authority figures and sense of self.

<u>As you consider the differences between Michael and Becky at age three, what are your thoughts?</u>

Becky at 6

- ➤ Becky is 6 years old.
- ➤ Her parents both work.
- ➤ Her grandma baby-sits her.
- ➤ She's in kindergarten.
- ➤ She is a very curious child.
- ➤ She has no siblings.
- ➤ Her parents, grandma and new teacher urge good behavior.
- ➤ They all use **The Box**, but family uses something else, too.

School can be a place for some kids to grow and succeed.

Becky is now in kindergarten. At first it was difficult for Becky, but of late she has gotten to know the ways of the teacher with the help of her parent's advice. The teacher has 24 in the class, which meets every afternoon. Grandma still baby-sits in the mornings.

When told of any problems in class, Becky's parents talk about it with her and warn her of what might happen if it continues -- and if it does, they will follow through as promised. When Becky gets into trouble before or after school, Grandma is careful not to punish her in ways that prevent her from having a normal day.

The routine in the evenings remains pretty much the same, but Becky's parents noticed more behavior problems when they first got home. She seemed glad to see them when they got home, but wanted more control of her own time. While they consistently punished inappropriate behavior, they took the time to find out why Becky wanted more freedom.

Bedtime continued to be no problem. But mornings were much more of a problem before her parents went to work. They decided that they needed to find out from her and grandma what was bothering Becky.

What they discovered had to do with her still trying to adjust to the demands of the kindergarten teacher and all the kids.

Becky still seems happy even when she seems stubbornly independent after school. Grandma is having the most trouble with Becky when she first gets home from school, which was perceived as Becky needing her freedom and regaining some sense of control over things. Grandma is careful to plan activities Becky can be in charge of.

Even though ***everyone used The Box***, Becky was already being given many freedoms.

<u>Write any additional thoughts here:</u>

Parents differ, and so do kids.

<u>Please think about and summarize in your own words what you feel are the differences between Michael and Becky at age 6, and why?</u>

<u>The strictness of Michael's parents is not that much different than Becky's – why, though, do we see Becky already thriving while Michael is fighting?</u>

Becky at 9

- ➢ Becky is 9 years old.
- ➢ Her parents both work.
- ➢ Her grandma baby-sits her.
- ➢ She's in the third grade.
- ➢ She is a very curious child.
- ➢ She has no siblings.
- ➢ Her parents, grandma and new teacher urge good behavior.
- ➢ They all use **The Box**, but many use something else, too.

Some kids are just good.

Or are they?

Becky is in the third grade, and is getting average grades. Her parents think she is doing much less well than she did in first and second grades. Her teacher says she shows effort but talks too much with other students when they are working. Becky says she likes her teacher -- "But she's too strict."

Grandma only baby-sits her when she gets home from school, and when her parents go out in the evenings or on weekends. She says Becky is easy to get along with no matter what is going on. She says that every once in a while she has to punish her for something, but it happening less and less over time. Grandma never sends her to her room or takes her afternoon snack away from her. Becky tells her parents that "Grandma gets upset sometimes, but I usually deserve it."

Becky's parents have noticed that even though they have to punish less frequently, they have to find higher levels of punishment than before. They feel that her occasional stubbornness and lies are natural stages she must go through, and have dedicated themselves to remain consistent and not let her get by with either one. They told Becky that she is a nicer person than that and that she will lose privileges every time she does such things in the future.

Her teacher tells her parents that they all need to be on the same page because next year in fourth grade schoolwork will get harder and Becky will need better study habits. Becky's parents support the teacher, but they also try to help the teacher see ways of working better with Becky.

Becky has mostly happy times, but there are a few moody times. Becky's parents and grandma try to remain supportive of good behavior in any case.

Please think about and summarize in your own words what you feel are the differences between Michael and Becky at age 9, and why?

Sometimes we think the answer lies in the fact that boys are different than girls – while that may be true, parenting methods still have dramatic effects on the cooperation children show towards authority figures. What do you think?

Becky at 15

- Becky is 15 years old.
- Her parents both work.
- Her grandma baby-sits her.
- She's in the ninth grade.
- She is a very curious youth.
- She has no siblings.
- Her parents, grandma and new teachers urge good behavior.
- They all use **The Box**, but many use something else, too.

Independence looks different when there is freedom.

Becky is in the ninth-grade and still gets slightly above-average grades, except that it's harder for her to keep them at that level. She complains that they don't explain things well enough and that they give unfair tests and too much homework. Her parents have remained steadfast in their encouragement of Becky to do the best she can, and they help her with her homework whenever needed. They told her that they would not set her homework schedule unless her grades started to fall.

Becky is more into friends than her schoolwork, especially her "skiing buddies". She and her friends get together or talk on the phone every day and evening. Sometimes the only time her parents see her is at dinner, when she does homework and chores, or during family activities. Her parents have long guided her about destruction of property, smoking and drugs -- things they've heard that "teenagers get into".

Becky's grandma is available to come over when she first gets home from school. She doesn't baby-sit days anymore, but occasionally comes over on weekends if Becky's parents go out of town. She and Becky interact a lot, but she does not try to establish Becky's activities. She tends to guide Becky rather than control her.

Becky's teachers feel she could try harder, but that she is not trouble in class. One teacher is aware that Becky is in a lot of sports and activities at school and very popular with her classmates. Becky's parents try to get to know all of her friends, and continue to support her avoidance of smoking and drugs. They believe her when she tells them where she goes and who she is with. If she doesn't tell them, or something happens differently, they remind her of the importance of trust if she wants more independence. Becky seems happy most of the time.

Write any additional thoughts here:

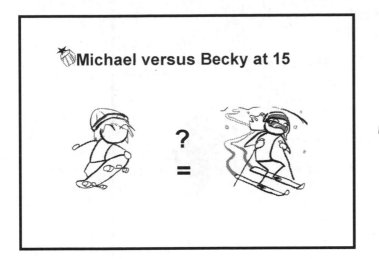

*Independence
is a desire
that begins
somewhere.*

<u>Please think about and summarize in your own words what you feel are
the differences between Michael and Becky at age 15, and why?</u>

<u>Remember, children and youth caught too often or too abusively in **The
Box** do not know it is **The Box** – they believe the problem is adults, and
they begin to go to one another for support and help – hence they begin
to shy away from parents and teachers for emotional support. What are
your thoughts?</u>

Becky at 18

> Becky is 18 years old.
> Her parents both work.
> She's about to graduate from high school *with honors*.
> She is a very curious youth.
> Her parents, grandma and new teachers urge good behavior.
> They all use *The Box*, but many use something else, too.

Going somewhere is easier when a person is in control.

Becky has a good chance of graduating from high school with honors. Her grades have steadily improved throughout high school, and she never had go to summer school. Her teachers say she tries hard, and wants to learn. While she is no particular behavior problem, she still talks a little too much in class with other students.

Becky's parents have worked hard to help her do better in school, but wanted her to sense her own accomplishments. They think it was important that they support all her activities, not just her academics.

As one teacher put it, "You don't have to keep after Becky -- she's motivated." Her parents agree; it seems that Becky thinks for herself. She never waits for others to dictate what she is supposed to do, unless she is unsure and then she asks for guidance so she can make her own decisions. The school counselor says it is the same way with her friends, "They cannot control what Becky does."

Becky is sometimes moody, closed off in her room listening to music or playing video games. She still has conversations with her mom or grandma. She and her dad have gotten a lot closer the last two years, and they get into meaningful discussions. Becky told the counselor that "I like it when people support me, and care what I think."

Becky goes out with a bunch of kids every Friday and Saturday night. They stay out late sometimes but not too late, and she sleeps in late afterwards. She has a part-time job, which she seems to like. She's been seeing a lot of one particular boy lately -- her parents seem to like him a lot. She seems totally excited about graduating and can't wait until next year and college.

Write any additional thoughts here:

A bright future
seems blinding
when we start
in darkness.

Please think about and summarize in your own words what you feel are the differences between Michael and Becky at age 18, and why?

Too frequent or too abusive uses of **_The Box_** creates behavior patterns that begin to define a person socially and academically – in essence, parents and teachers begin to expect little or a lot based on prior performance and the cooperation they get from the child or youth. What do you think?

Becky at 20

- ➢ Becky is 20 years old.
- ➢ She is doing well in college.
- ➢ She is on scholarship.
- ➢ Her parents both work.
- ➢ She is a very confident student.
- ➢ Her parents, grandma and professors encourage good work.
- ➢ They all use *The Box*, but many use something else, too.

Achieving goals typically leads to more goals.

Becky graduated with honors, and got a small scholarship to college. Her parents suggested that she take a short summer program to strengthen her study skills before college, since she tends to be in so many activities. She completed the program, and then went on to college.

The boy he has been seeing lately is getting serious. She hasn't decided if she likes him that much or not, and has asked him to back off; but they still date. Becky is more worried that they'll both leave college if they get too serious.

Becky has changed her major field of study. She had wanted to be a teacher -- "I could do better than most of the one's I had." But now she wants to become a lawyer, primarily because of her ability to think things through and work with people. She runs around with a bunch of new kids she met in college -- that's how he met the current boyfriend.

She thanks her parents for being so supportive, and still turns to them when she needs good advice. She says that too many of her teachers, especially in high school, were not good teachers and that it was lucky she was motivated to learn. She hopes someday with her law degree to be able to influence legislation to improve teaching.

Becky acts very happy go lucky when you see her with friends and family. She gets moody or stressed sometimes when there are some heavy exams or projects due at school, or when she and her boyfriend argue. But once the crisis is past she is herself.

Because of the scholarship, Becky is able to have a car, which makes it easier for her to get back and forth to school and to her part-time job. She handles things very well.

<u>Write any additional thoughts here:</u>

Please think about and summarize in your own words what you feel are the differences between Michael and Becky at age 20, and why?

As a person is continually caught in **The Box**, he/she begins to develop a dependency on "playing the game" rather than become self-motivated, waiting to be nudged, urged or forced by others to do things. What do you think?

Becky at 26

- Becky is 26 years old.
- Law school is interesting and stressful.
- She is happily married.
- She is a very confident woman.
- Her parents, grandma and professors encourage good work.
- They all use **The Box**, but many use something else, too.

Life can be a wondrous adventure, even with problems.

Becky is just completing law school, which is a little later than planned because she and her boyfriend of many years got married. He is a teacher and has been teaching for four years. She worked for a while to help them buy a home, and then went back to grad-school.

Becky is very stressed with the difficult projects finishing up law school. Her husband is very supportive, and balances their time together to keep from adding to her stress.

She only gets together with his parents for holidays and occasional weekends. Her parents always ask how she's doing, which she views as willingness to support her if needed. She feels free to honestly tell them, knowing full well they will not try to run her life.

Except for her husband, whom she believes is "true blue", Becky has real doubts about herself and the future. Her husband tells her that it is just a phase all finishing law students go through. They have a close relationship, and talk things through together.

Becky is happy when she is with friends, which helps to forget the press of law school. Over the years, she and her husband have been careful to associate with friends who are careful about drinking and do not use drugs. It has paid off many times, as they have been able to count on their friends in times of need.

Becky thinks about the future all the time -- she hopes to make a difference. She also hopes to have children/youth and a happy family life like her parents. She also hopes she can be as good of a parent as her parents.

Despite all the stress of law school, Becky is a happy woman.

Write any additional thoughts here:

Bored workers come in all kinds of clothing.

Please think about and summarize in your own words what you feel are the differences between Michael and Becky at age 26, and why?

Just as children and youth caught in *The Box* beginning to blame adults, adults, too, blame other adults. What do you think?

Becky at 40

- ➢ Becky is 40 years old.
- ➢ She has moved up in her job.
- ➢ Her marriage is fulfilling.
- ➢ Her parents are retired.
- ➢ Her grandma is in a nursing home.
- ➢ She is a very successful person.
- ➢ Her parents, grandma and boss encourage good work.
- ➢ They all use **The Box**, but many use something else, too.

Maturation is a never-ending process.

Becky completed law school and became a competent lawyer. After she became a partner in her law firm, she took four years off to have two children/youth. She has recently accepted the challenge of entering local politics, still wanting to improve schools.

Her marriage is good. The kids are 4 and 6 years old, and her husband feels they can handle him going to graduate school full-time to finish his Master's Degree. She has met someone who is ready to back her political campaign, and she is ready to move on to better things. Becky seems very capable of balancing motherhood, being a good wife and dedication to her own career.

Becky and her husband have kept up their relationships with good friends, and have expanded that ring of friends over the years. However, they have never allowed those friends to take precedence over their children/youth. She and her husband spend many hours with their kids, playing, guiding, supporting and loving.

Becky's parents are proud of Becky. Her parents feel Becky is fortunate to have such a supportive husband. They spend a lot of time with Becky and her family. They do the occasional "baby-sitter thing" which they view as fun, but Becky views as providing a family foundation -- she wants her children/youth to have the same wisdom and support she herself got as a child.

Becky is still as idealistic as she was entering college. Despite the stresses of modern times, she is a confident, competent woman who knows the value of supportive family members, friends and colleagues. She is looking forward to the future, and knows deep down within herself that she can make a difference.

<u>Write any additional thoughts here:</u>

Maturation is a never-ending process, except for victims.

Please think about and summarize in your own words what you feel are the differences between Michael and Becky, and why?

People caught in ***The Box*** frequently [or abusively] begin eventually to feel like victims. Feeling victimized is a horrible place to be. What do you think?

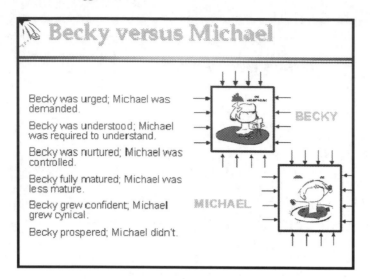

The Michael example offers somewhat of an insight on what a **Steady Diet of The Box** [parents and adults who over-control a child/youth] can do to stifle maturation. The Becky example offers somewhat of an insight on what **parenting beyond The Box** can do to encourage maturation.

Do you know anyone who seemed to mature faster and better than someone else? If so, please describe the differences in how they were treated as they grew up:

Then, how were they treated as an adult?

Parenting, teaching and managing beyond **The Box** helps people become self-motivated beyond just winning in **The Box**.

MYSELF BEYOND *The Box*

Learning to live *Beyond The Box*

THE CHILD'S FUTURE

There has to be something more than "Boxes"!

AS A FUTURE ADULT
➤ Finding Healthy Boxes
➤ Coping in Healthy Boxes
➤ Avoiding Unhealthy Boxes
➤ Coping in Unhealthy Boxes
➤ Finding trust & relevance
➤ Giving trust & relevance

Mid-life crisis is realizing that trading Boxes and winning in them is not enough.

There has to be more to life than The Box

As we provide enough <u>trust and relevance</u>, we can openly discuss with our child/youth how to cope with *The Boxes* they will face as an adult. We can help them in:

Finding Healthy Boxes. We can help them learn how to think through their choices of friends, activities, education and jobs.

Coping in Healthy Boxes. We can help them maintain healthy habits at school, in their relationships, on-the-job and at home.

Avoiding Unhealthy Boxes. We can help them identify and avoid peers who will pull them down, activities that are dangerous, violent or unlawful, drugs/alcohol.

Coping in Unhealthy Boxes. We can help them handle themselves when they get caught up in a bad situation, and help them find a way out.

Finding trust & relevance. We can help them be able to quickly distinguish between over-controlling, artificial and superficial relationships versus truly intimate ones.

Giving trust & relevance. We can help them give to others what they want in return, and to be able find balanced relationships with honest, healthy "give and take".

IMPORTANT: Parents, who take this aspect of parenting seriously, leave a lot less to chance. The two-way discussions we have with our children/youth as they grow up tend to set their moral and ethical values. We need to plan carefully how to guide our child's look at *Future Boxes*, and to face them ourselves as we live our lives in front of them as their "role model". So, <u>we do that best by seeking and maintaining an atmosphere of **trust and relevance**!</u>

<u>Write any additional thoughts here:</u>

```
┌─────────────────────────────────────────────┐
│                                               │
│        COPING WITH *My Boxes*                 │
│                                               │
│                                               │
│        As A Person Living Beyond *The Box*    │
│                                               │
│              Family Member                    │
│                 Student                       │
│                  Friend                       │
│                 Citizen                       │
│                 Spouse                        │
│                 Parent                        │
│                Co-worker                      │
│                 Leader                        │
│                Influence                      │
│                                               │
└─────────────────────────────────────────────┘
```

Where are we? We tend to function in several ways during our lives. We conduct ourselves according to our view of ourselves, often referred to as "self-esteem". **The Box** is a major factor in growing up and the development of our self-esteem.

❑ If we have learned to "play the game" in **The Box**, we view ourselves based on the degree to which we "win versus lose" at <u>pleasing others</u>.

❑ If we have learned to "use" **The Box**, we view ourselves based on the percentage of times we "win versus lose" at <u>controlling others</u>.

For each function we play in life, we could separate ourselves according to whether or not we are being controlled or are doing the controlling. We would limit how we look at these functions in this way if we have become dependent on **The Box**. There is a basic rule of thumb:

People brought-up in The Box, usually
depend on The Box later in life!

Since most people encounter *The Box* heavily from parents and teachers, most people have a dependency on it to some degree or another. This leads to a basic question:

How well do I cope with my Boxes?

How well do I cope when others use *The Box* on me? How well do I use *The Box* when I try to control others? Do I find myself dealing with *The Box* most of the time?

<u>Write any additional thoughts here:</u>

WHY ME?

Boxed-in Parents
Tend to *Box-in* Children

➤ The fast-paced world we live in and work is causing a lot of stress.

➤ Our current stress level impacts how we treat our children.

➤ The methods of our own parents and teachers leave lasting marks on us.

➤ Our self esteem becomes the driving force.

Boxed-in parents have little time to parent;

So they use The Box because it's fast and easy.

The fast-paced world we live in and work is causing a lot of stress. With single parent homes or both parents working, children and youth often have parents or guardians who have significantly higher stress levels than are deemed to be healthy. The problems children and youth have with friends and at school only add to the stress as parents. There is a lot on the line when we take on the job of parenting. A large part of the reason we are stressed out to begin with is because we feel ***boxed-in*** ourselves.

Our current stress level impacts how we treat our children/youth. When we are angry, frustrated, or fearful we tend to use more of the punishing side of ***The Box***. We tend to stubbornly hold onto our own view of what children and youth should be doing or not doing, and we become impatient and dictatorial -- we become our child's "worst nightmare".

The methods of our own parents and teachers leave lasting marks on us. Almost as important as our stress level are the methods we learned from our own parents and teachers as they told us what to do, offered rewards and/or threatened punishment, and tried to manipulate us into feeling like we were having a good time. To the degree we are a product of ***The Box***, our first inclinations will be to use it [and only it] with our children. When mixed with stress, ***The Box*** can become abusive:

- ❑ We punish too severely and withhold rewards altogether.
- ❑ We use it over and over again -- a ***Steady Diet of The Box*** is abusive.

Our self-esteem becomes the driving force. The bottom line to parenting is what we think of ourselves. If we feel non-acceptable or perfect, we can go too far in one of two ways:

- ❑ Push children and youth too hard -- use ***The Box*** too much or too harshly.
- ❑ Neglect children and youth too much -- don't use ***The Box*** enough -- no boundaries.

Our boxes often cause stress THEY impact our parenting APPROACH

```
┌─────────────────────────────────────────────┐
│                                               │
│   COPING WITH My Boxes                        │
│                                               │
│                                               │
│                   AS A PARENT                 │
│            ┌──────────────────────────┐       │
│            │ ➤ Am I "boxed in"?        │       │
│            └──────────────────────────┘       │
│            ❑ Finding Healthy Boxes.           │
│            ❑ Coping in Healthy Boxes.         │
│            ❑ Avoiding Unhealthy Boxes.        │
│            ❑ Coping in Unhealthy Boxes.       │
│                                               │
└─────────────────────────────────────────────┘
```

Sometimes people are so boxed-in they don't know it.

Being a parent is probably the most important endeavor we undertake. The future of society rests with the results of how we succeed with this task. Successful parents point with pride that ***they have helped guarantee the security and happiness of:***

- ❑ *Their children*
- ❑ *Themselves*
- ❑ *And society as a whole*

Is this what you want to achieve as a parent? Write in your own words what you want:

Since parenting is such an important responsibility, it is essential for parents to find physical and emotional "well-being" for themselves. As a parent, we need to learn how to cope with **The Boxes** affecting our lives. In order to do this, we must first identify which **Boxes** impact our lives the most. We need to identify:

❑ ***Boxes*** that impacted us in the past

❑ ***Boxes*** that are currently impacting us now

On the next page you will find a brief questionnaire which is designed to help you identify ***Healthy and Unhealthy Boxes*** from the past and now. Please complete the questionnaire:

WHERE AM I *"Boxed-In"*?

Where do I feel *"boxed-in"*, and how does it affect my happiness?

For each area, circle if you are boxed-in: Past (P), <u>and/or</u> Current (C) <u>or</u> Never (N).
Then, circle how you currently feel: Happy (H),   Somewhat Happy (S), <u>or</u> Unhappy (U).

✓	My relationship(s) with my significant other(s)?	P C N	H S U
✓	My relationships with my parents and siblings?	P C N	H S U
✓	My relationships with my friends?	P C N	H S U
✓	My work situations?	P C N	H S U
✓	My financial situation?	P C N	H S U
✓	My schooling and educational level?	P C N	H S U
✓	Certain religious or spiritual situations?	P C N	H S U
✓	My relationship with other children I've parented?	P C N	H S U
✓	My relationship with myself?	P C N	H S U
✓	My physical and emotional health?	P C N	H S U

Sorting out where we are boxed-in helps us separate things into manageable pieces.

Please circle answers for each of the above questions based on <u>how you feel at this time</u>. It is normal to feel somewhat ***"boxed-in"*** by things from the past as well as now. There are no right or wrong answers. What you actually feel is clearly the most important answer. <u>Please circle your answers as follows; circle</u>:

    [P] -- for the areas that boxed you in during the <u>past</u>

    [C] -- for the areas that are boxing you in <u>currently</u>

    [N] -- for the areas that have <u>never</u> boxed you in

Circle both, if both apply.

<u>Then circle how healthy you feel about each one at this time; circle</u>:

    [H] -- for the areas you currently feel <u>happy</u>

    [S] -- for the areas you currently feel <u>somewhat happy</u>

    [U] -- for the areas you currently feel <u>unhappy</u>

<u>Now, please describe below your current level of happiness, and why:</u>

If you feel like you have always been ***Boxed-in*** and/or feel overly boxed-in now, and it is making you consistently unhappy, some type of professional counseling might help.

<u>Write any additional thoughts here:</u>

IMPACT ON PARENTING

Do *My Boxes* impact how I parent?

- ➢ What are my prior models of how to parent?
- ➢ What are the "rules" that I've learned to live by?
- ➢ How much time do I have to actively parent?
- ➢ How much do relationships impact me as a parent?
- ➢ How much does my stress level impact me as a parent?

Being too boxed in can make us feel guilty about our parenting.

Answer the following questions even if you are not a parent ...

What are my prior models of how to parent?

What are the "rules" that I've learned to live by?

How much time do I have to actively parent?

How much do relationships impact me as a parent?

How much does my current stress level impact me as a parent?

Again, if you feel currently overwhelmed by past or current **Boxes**, it might be beneficial to seek out a professional counselor.

Write any additional thoughts here:

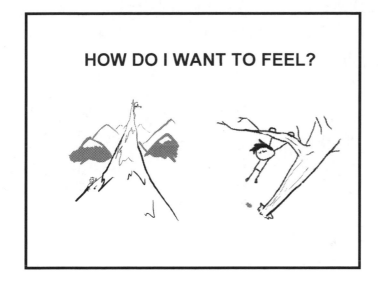

HOW DO I WANT TO FEEL?

Feelings drives what we do, or what we don't do.

FEELING "ON TOP OF THINGS"

When things are going well, and we feel "on top of things", our energy level is high, and our attitude is good. We seem to be motivated in the right directions, and things seem to "fall into place" and problems tend "to work themselves out". We have courage when needed, yet we remain aware of and accepting of our limitations.

Describe the last stretch of time when you felt "on top of things":

FEELING "OUT ON A LIMB"

When things seem to always be going wrong, our energy is sapped and our attitude can slip. We seem less motivated, or motivated in the wrong directions. We can get very angry and frustrated, and if the anger doesn't work we can find ourselves left with no way to turn or any idea on how to work things out.

Describe the last stretch of time when you felt "out on a limb".

COPING WITH *My* Boxes

AS A PARENT

☑ AM I "boxed in"?

➤ Finding Healthy Boxes.

❑ Coping in Healthy Boxes.

❑ Avoiding Unhealthy Boxes.

❑ Coping in Unhealthy Boxes.

Knowing that the rules of the game are "fair" helps us succeed in The Box, and outside it.

*What does a **Healthy Box** look like -- what are the basic criteria?*

- ❑ It does not try to force you to go against your basic beliefs and values.
- ❑ It does not constantly possess and manipulate you.
- ❑ It lets you negotiate the rules, and defend yourself if rules are broken or bent.
- ❑ It does not abuse you.
- ❑ It always modifies itself for mutual comfort and "well-being".
- ❑ The person using **The Box** is fair, kind, sensitive, and considerate.
- ❑ The person tightens or loosens **The Box** based on mutual needs and desires.

What else would you add to the *criteria for a **Healthy Box**?*

It is extremely important to add that we can become too dependent on a **Healthy Box**, and can actually make it unhealthy for us.

Since everyone uses **The Box** to some degree, it is important to search for people and situations that will not overly **Box** us in. Whether it is family members at home, or bosses, employees and customers at work, or friends and family outside of home, or situations providing education, entertainment or recreation, we need to be clear about the above *criteria for a **Healthy Box**.* Our own health depends on it.

Write any additional thoughts here:

FINDING *Healthy Boxes*

The 9-Step Process

1. Define the target situation
2. Set "healthy criteria"
3. Place myself near target
4. Get in there and try
5. Remain who you are
6. Keep my values
7. Assess the situation
8. Weigh against the "criteria"
9. Stay or move on

Know what you are looking for, think it through carefully, and go for it.

1. **DEFINE THE TARGET SITUATION:** what general type of relationship do you need? Are you looking for another friend, a recreation buddy, a new church, a new job, etc.?

2. **SET "HEALTHY CRITERIA":** what are the things that would be necessary to make this a healthy relationship, such as physical and emotional characteristics, activities and behaviors expected, type of personalities involved, etc.?

3. **PLACE MYSELF NEAR TARGET:** where do I need to go in order for me to meet this person or get acquainted with an organization. Maybe I can narrow down the list of possibilities against the "healthy criteria" even before I put myself in the situation:

4. **GET IN THERE AND TRY:** what will motivate me to go there and "hang in there" as I review the situation and person(s) involved? What are the obstacles, such as money, time, distance, clothes to wear, energy level, etc.; and how can I overcome them?

5. **REMAIN WHO YOU ARE:** who am I? Can I be myself? Do I have to put on an act?

6. **KEEP MY VALUES:** can I live in the situation and retain my own value system?

7. **ASSESS THE SITUATION:** am I willing to stay in or return to the situation for a long enough time to look at it objectively? Will I stay too long; or run too soon?

8. **WEIGH AGAINST THE "CRITERIA":** am I rigorous enough in my assessment to weigh the situation back against my "healthy criteria"? Should seek counsel or advice?

9. **STAY OR MOVE ON:** from the outset -- will I be able to "walk away" if the situation does not live up to the criteria I set for a healthy relationship? It finally comes down to a basic question -- does (or will) the relationship allow me to remain healthy?

<u>Write any additional thoughts here:</u>

FINDING *Healthy Boxes*

Defining The Situation

1. Define the target situation
2. Set "healthy criteria"
3. Place myself near target
4. Get in there and try
5. Remain who you are
6. Keep my values
7. Assess the situation
8. Weigh against the "criteria"
9. Stay or move on

Knowing what is healthy for you is the key

Finding *Healthy Boxes* is important throughout our lives. It takes on extra importance following someone's death, a divorce, the loss of a job, our children leaving the nest, major illness, or the breakup of an important relationship. We are especially vulnerable to looking for the dependencies we had before. Starting anew is an opportunity to break free from any unhealthy tendencies in our previous situation. Too often though, we are aware of this only at the feeling level and do not have a logical plan to truly get what we want.

The nine steps at the top suggest that we can search for *Healthy Boxes* in a logical fashion. Getting started means using steps 1 & 2 above to describe relationships you might want to seek out, such as finding a friend at work or in your church, a new golfing or tennis partner, or a neighbor.

Describe below a new type of relationship you might need:

<u>Define target situation: the type of new relationship you are seeking:</u>

<u>List healthy criteria: things you feel are necessary for it to be a healthy relationship:</u>

FINDING *Healthy Boxes*

Completing A Plan

1. Define the target situation
2. Set "healthy criteria"
3. Place myself near target
4. Get in there and try
5. Remain who you are
6. Keep my values
7. Assess the situation
8. Weigh against the "criteria"
9. Stay or move on

You can't swim without jumping into the water.

OPTION: if the potential relationship you described on the previous page is important to you, then draft the remaining steps of your 9-step plan here:

3. How to place myself near target:

4. How to get in there and try:

5. How to remain who you are:

6. How to keep my values:

7. How to assess the situation:

8. How to assure myself to weigh it against "healthy criteria":

9. How to stay or move on:

Other:

FINDING *Healthy Boxes*

Seeking Advice & Counsel

➤ Share plan with people you know and trust; who you feel are objective.
➤ Talk with them from time-to-time as you are looking into the situation.
➤ Remember, old memories can impact your decision making -- so be careful.
➤ Professional counselor?

Seeking help is a sign of strength, not weakness.

If you are seeking an important relationship, one which could impact your physical and emotional well-being, then it may be important to have someone help you through all or part of the 9-step process.

Share plan with people you know and trust -- those you feel can be objective. If you are inclined to do this on a regular, informal basis as part of regular conversation, you might want to pick a time and place more conducive to showing a person that this is important to you. Pick someone you like and trust who will keep it confidential, and who will try to help you be objective.

Talk with them from time-to-time as you are looking into the situation. If the situation is fairly complex, it may take days or weeks to work through it. If it is finding a long-term relationship, it may take even longer. Talk with the person or people as you feel you need to in order to sort things out.

Remember, old memories can impact your decision-making -- so be careful. All of us have the tendencies to see what want to see or be afraid to see what is really there. These tendencies can get us into relationships that look healthy but aren't; or they can prevent us from forming a relationship that would have been good for us.

Nelson L. Noggle, Ph.D.

Professional counselor? If we tend to make the same mistakes over and over, such as getting into the same type of unhealthy relationships, or running away from them, we would likely benefit from seeking help from a professional counselor. There are all kinds of counselors -- financial advisors, job counselors, social workers, psychologists, church counselors, physical therapists, etc. Remember, though, professional help is another healthy relationship that has to be formed. Get one you can trust.

<u>Write any additional thoughts here:</u>

COPING WITH *My* Boxes

AS A PARENT

☑ Am I "boxed in"?
☑ Finding Healthy Boxes.
➤ Coping in Healthy Boxes.
❑ Avoiding Unhealthy Boxes.
❑ Coping in Unhealthy Boxes.

A box is a box.

In each there are rules of the game.

When we are in ***Healthy Boxes*** we sometimes tend to take things for granted. Why?

Coping in a ***Healthy Box*** is just as important as coping in an unhealthy one, for three important reasons:

❑ We don't want to become too dependent on ***The Box***.
❑ We don't want to turn it into an ***Unhealthy Box***.
❑ We don't want to destroy our relationship with the person using ***The Box***.

Here are some ideas for learning how to cope in a ***Healthy Box***:

❑ *Know what **The Box** is* -- understand the directions, rewards, punishment and entertainment that are being used to define the relationship or situation.
❑ *Treat it as a contract* -- know what you have to give and get in order to keep relationship or situation healthy.

❏ *Remember this is only* **One Box** -- there are many other relationships and situations in your life -- this is only one of them.

❏ *Rely on it for what it is* -- stay aware of the nature of the contract and avoid trying to make it more than it is or allowing it to absorb other aspects of your life.

❏ *Avoid blind trust* -- since it is a contract, settle all disputes accordingly and re-negotiate the nature of contract as needed; its health is continually defined.

<u>Write any additional thoughts here:</u>

COPING IN A *Healthy Box*

➢ Knowing the current "contract"
- Directions
- Rewards
- Punishment
- Entertainment

➢ Re-negotiating the "contract"
- My view
- Their view
- Communication
- Mutual commitment

The rules of the game are a contract.

The temptation is to blindly enter into relationship. My mother-in-law offered these wise words before I married her daughter:

Love is blind, but marriage is an eye opener!

Write what you think the contract is for one relationship you are in:

My View	Their View
DIRECTIONS [What I'm supposed to do.]	DIRECTIONS [What they're supposed to do.]
REWARDS [What I get from the reationship.]	REWARS [What they get from the relationship]
PUNISHMENT [What I have to put up with.]	PUNISHMENT [What they have to put up with.]
ENTERTAINMENT [The fun for me.]	ENTERTAINMENT [The fun for them.]

Do you like what you see? If not, it may be time to re-negotiate it.

Communication keeps things fair and just.

CHANGE IS NOT ALWAYS NECESSARY WITH GOOD COMMUNICATION

As we closely review the nature of a relationship, and look at its stated or implied contract, many times it is OK to keep things as they already are. As individuals grow and mature during a relationship, an ongoing healthy communication can keep the relationship intact and feeling healthy.

<u>Describe the ways in which one of your more healthy relationships seems to adapt and stay healthy through good communication:</u>

JUSTICE AND FAIRNESS PREVAILS

When we look at relationships that have good communication, we tend to find that each person feels that they are treating one another in a just and fair manner. Coping in a healthy relationship seems to be a matter of keeping selfishness at a minimum and looking out for each other's interests without controlling one another.

<u>List the areas in the above relationship where this type of fairness most often occurs:</u>

COPING WITH *My* Boxes

AS A PARENT

☑ Am I "boxed in"?

☑ Finding Healthy Boxes.

☑ Coping in Healthy Boxes.

➢ Avoiding Unhealthy Boxes.

❑ Coping in Unhealthy Boxes.

Unhealthy boxes drain us of energy and patience

It is important to stay or get away from *Unhealthy Boxes.* They can place an enormous emotional weight on you. Note -- some *Boxes* are not people:

❑ Possessive or abusive loved ones, friends, teachers, bosses, etc.

❑ Unrewarding and dead-end jobs or careers

❑ Addiction to work, parties, sexual affairs, alcohol, drugs, etc.

❑ Overly dogmatic religious leaders and organizations

❑ Compulsive reactions to certain people and situations

❑ Self-inflicted attitudes about oneself

Earlier, you assessed how *Boxed-in* you feel. How could you have avoided any of those things? Given the fact that hindsight is almost perfect, what might you have done differently about some of them?

Recalling how too much of *The Box* creates dependent and co-dependent behaviors, we need to think things through carefully before getting into a *New Box.* We need to be able to see the trap before we fall into it ...

AVOIDING *Unhealthy Boxes*

1-9. Use the 9-step Process
10. Clearly predict the "contract"
11. Avoid dependent situations
12. Avoid playing to addictions
13. Weigh against other *boxes*
14. Estimate the effort needed
15. Limit "fix me" situations
16. Limit "fix them" situations
17. Who stands to gain most?

Knowing what you don't want is as important as knowing what you do want.

If we are honest with ourselves, and sometimes we need someone to help us achieve that, we can logically overcome an impulsive desire to get into a bad situation. Even if our own dependencies are steering us in the wrong direction, we can learn to depend on a business-like process of looking at the situation objectively.

After the first 8 steps of the *9-Step Process* (page 176), we can predict what the *Box-like Contract* would look like. After that, we need to "judge" the situation so we can:

Avoid dependent situations -- stay out of situations that "play to" my self-esteem needs and/or theirs.

Avoid playing to addictions -- stay out of situations that enable either of us to fulfill our addictive needs.

Weigh against other boxes -- stay out of situations that look too much like other unhealthy situations that have hurt us before.

Estimate the effort needed -- stay out of situations that require too much work to constantly keep the situation tolerable.

Limit "fix me" or "fix-them" situations -- do not make helping one another the main goal of the relationship; keep that in balance with other major reasons to be together.

Who stands to gain the most? Stay away from situations where one person constantly gets a lot more out of it than someone else; they tend to become unhealthy.

> ***Preventing unhealthy situations may be
> easier than dealing with them.***

<u>Write any additional thoughts here:</u>

IT'S OK TO BE PICKY

Beware of advice, especially if it helps you see things as you want to see them.

Beware of initial infatuation and the "honeymoon period" of "surface intimacy".

Never back off of your high standards.

STAY PICKY

When you have clearly defined the criteria for a relationship, stick to them. While you are not looking for perfection, you are looking for mutual trust and respect. Healthy relationships grow through fairly predictable phases, hopefully maturing from initial infatuation into a long-lasting period of harmony and intimacy. If any one individual continues to seduce, manipulate, control or seek to change the other(s), the health of the existing and future relationship is in question. Find out if the behavior of another person is truly the kind of person he/she can be over the long haul. Can they sustain their "glow" or is it just part of a courting period after which everything will change? Be careful of advice from others. Watch-out for seeing things through rose-colored glasses and seeing things the way you want to see them. Don't fall for surface qualities that have little to do with intimate, trustful and respectful communication. Stay picky -- do not settle for something less than you want -- you are worth it.

TAKE YOUR TIME

Be careful to take your time in forming a new relationship. There is no need to hurry -- the time lost in trying to fix and exit a bad relationship easily outweighs the time you could have spent being more careful in the beginning. ***You don't want to jump from One Box to another!***

Describe a relationship in which you feel you jumped into it too fast -- and what eventually happened:

COPING WITH *My* Boxes

AS A PARENT

☑ Am I "boxed in"?
☑ Finding Healthy Boxes.
☑ Coping in Healthy Boxes.
☑ Avoiding Unhealthy Boxes.
➤ Coping in Unhealthy Boxes.

We must survive, because we are worth it.

Sometimes we find ourselves in an ***Unhealthy Box***, but it is not easy to get out. We cannot always give up a relationship or get out of a situation that easily. It is about all we can do just to cope.

First, what do you think are the reasons people stay in an ***Unhealthy Box?***

Second, what has to happen to make them leave an ***Unhealthy Box?***

Third, what could an ***Unhealthy Box*** do to a person's self-esteem?

The toughest decision sometimes is whether or not to get out of an ***Unhealthy Box***. If we cannot get what we want and need, we can get caught in the endless cycle of trying to redefine the "rules" rather than get out. This is another time professional counseling can help -- sorting out the pluses and minuses of staying or leaving ***The Box.***

COPING IN *Unhealthy Boxes*

HELP!

COPE OR GET OUT

➤ Review the "contract"
➤ Identify any unmet criteria
➤ Where else can criteria be met
➤ Is what's left good enough
➤ If so, re-negotiate "contract"
➤ If not, create transition plan
➤ Regardless, don't let things get
  any worse

*Get out if you
can, and cope
until you do.*

The <u>emotional overload</u> of an ***Unhealthy Box*** prevents us from looking at situations in a business-like manner. We tend to lose all logic, and get caught up in our Fight-Flight stress reactions instead. One way of logically proceeding would be to us the *9-Step Process* (page 176) to look at a current situation as if it were new. Another sequence is suggested above beginning with a review of the contract. In either case, a person needs to be objective enough to face the possibility of getting out of the situation.

The contract and any unmet criteria -- one of the major problems with typical unhealthy situations is that a contract has never been created, or at best each person has a vague notion of what they want from the relationship. Regardless, a person needs to objectively look at <u>all</u> the unmet needs and desires (criteria) for a healthy relationship. The next concern has to do where can those needs be met, and whether or not the current relationship can become healthier if the needs and desires are met elsewhere? Sometimes, re-negotiating the contract can salvage an unhealthy situation.

<u>Do you have a potentially unhealthy relationship or situation that you need to resolve? If so, feel free to use the format suggested on page 185</u>

to review and revise the contract. Note here any thoughts you may have about coping, resolving, or getting out of it:

*Living and parenting are hard enough when things are normal!
We don't need Unhealthy Boxes hanging
around our necks as we try to do them.*

GETTING OUT

➢ Elements of a Transition Plan
 × Timeline for getting out
 × Ways to "ease out"
 × Keeping safe in the meantime
 × Ways to leave "cold turkey"
 × Safe place(s) to go
➢ Considering All the People
 × Those I am running away from
 × Those I am protecting
 × Those who are helping or care
 × Myself

Cold turkey can work sometimes, but a plan helps make it happen more smoothly.

Elements of a Transition Plan -- another problem in unhealthy situations is when there is no safe plan for getting out. If the person judges the situation is too unhealthy, it is essential for them to logically plan their way out so that things do not get worse. In some instances, easing ones way out is best, which sets a timeline that minimizes the loss felt by all parties. Other times a quick or "cold-turkey" exit is best -- but we should never run away from something without a safe place to go -- no matter what, we do not want make things worse.

Considering All the People -- even when we want to get out of a relationship we may not want to hurt or anger the person(s) we're are running away from, for two possible reasons: (1) they may get back at us somehow, or (2) we just don't want to hurt or anger them. Yet, if we are going to leave, there will some type of impact on them that we must prepare ourselves to handle. If we are leaving to protect others, we have to think of how they will be impacted as well. Also, those who are helping us leave or care about our situation will be impacted. But, if we are not careful, we could forget the most important person -- the one needing to get out -- ourselves.

<u>Do you have any relationship or situation that is preventing you from being a good parent or from doing a good job? Are you too **Boxed-in**? If so, what do you need to do?</u>

AM I HEALTHY ENOUGH?

Where do I feel *"boxed-in"*; do I need to change things?

For each item below, circle if you need to change things: Yes (Y), No (N), Maybe (M)

✓ Change my relationship(s) with my significant other(s)?   Y N M
✓ Change my relationships with my parents and siblings?   Y N M
✓ Change my relationships with my friends?   Y N M
✓ Change my work situations?   Y N M
✓ Change my financial situations?   Y N M
✓ Change my schooling and educational level?   Y N M
✓ Change religious or spiritual situations?   Y N M
✓ Change my relationship with other children I've parented?   Y N M
✓ Change my relationship with myself?   Y N M
✓ Change my physical and emotional health?   Y N M

Emotional and physical health is a worthy goal.

Please circle answers for each of the above questions based on <u>how you feel at this time</u>. It is normal to feel somewhat ***"boxed-in"*** by things. There are no right or wrong answers. What you actually feel is clearly the most important answer. Please circle your answers for each of the above items as follows; circle:

❑ [Y] = <u>Yes</u> -- things do need to change

❑ [N] = <u>No</u> -- things do not need to change

❑ [M] = <u>Maybe</u> -- things may have to change

<u>Now please describe below your current priorities for becoming more emotionally and physically healthy so that you can accomplish the job of parenting.</u>

If you feel like you have always been ***Boxed-in*** and/or feel overly ***Boxed-in*** now, and it is making you consistently unhappy, some type of professional counseling might help.

DO I NEED A COUNSELOR?

**Seeking
Professional Counsel**

➤ Share plan with people
you know and trust; who
you feel are objective.

➤ Talk with them from time-
to-time as you are looking
into the situation.

➤ Remember, old memories
can impact your decision
making -- so be careful.

➤ Professional counselor?

*Good
counselors set
a tone of trust
and relevance,
just like we
need to for a
person under
our care.*

If you continue to have work-related problems, are having marital difficulties, seem to continually lose friends, tend to have too much trouble as a parent or are always getting into bad relationships, you may want to select a professional counselor. Here are some specific guidelines:

Share plan with people you know and trust -- those who you feel are objective. Finding a good counselor is actually the biggest step you can take to helping yourself return to a healthy frame of mind. The first counselor you see might not be the one <u>you</u> need; it is important to look for two things: (1) do they make you feel safe, and (2) do they deal with what is important to you? When you see a counselor, you are looking also at your relationship with yourself.

Talk with them from time-to-time as you are looking into the situation. If the situation is fairly complex, it may take weeks or months to work through it. Regular weekly sessions are the usual way it precedes, but counselors will meet with you at other times or more frequently as needed.

Remember, old memories can impact your decision-making -- so be careful. This is one of the specialties of many professional counselors.

Learning how to prevent past experiences from sabotaging current and future relationships is the goal.

Professional counselor? There are all kinds of counselors. Be sure to pick one who addresses what you want them to address. You might start out seeking help from a financial counselor, only to find out you also need a marital counselor. The main thing to remember -- you do not have to go back after the first meeting or two -- you are in charge of picking who you want to counsel you. It is essential that you feel safe and can deal with the issue(s) you want to address. You must first seek help to get it.

Getting help from the wrong person may only place you in *Another Box*.

Write any additional thoughts here:

WHAT COUNSELORS DO

To avoid the inquisition ....
To avoid demands ....

Counselors establish ....

☺ a **trusting environment** for the client, which is maintained at all times.

☺ **personal relevance** to the client, which is pursued at all times.

☺ **either one** at any given time, which helps cause and maintain the other.

Sometimes we cannot help others, such as our child, until we get help ourselves.

Counselors often succeed where friends or family members cannot. The reason for this is because counselors know that:

❑ By providing a *trusting environment*, a person will feel safe and free to discuss and deal with what is important to them -- *trust leads to relevance*.

❑ By dealing with what is *relevant* to a person, they feel that what is important to them is important also to the counselor -- *relevance leads to trust*.

❑ It doesn't matter which is established first, trust or relevance, *one tends to lead to the other* and stimulates and nurtures understanding and growth.

Write any additional thoughts here:

What is gained if a person feels free to go to someone and feels safe enough to talk about whatever is going on in their lives?

- ❑ What's gained for the person?

- ❑ What's gained for the person doing the counseling?

- ❑ What's gained for their relationship?

- ❑ How does a person's peers provide this (which can be both good and bad)?

***Remember, <u>TRUST AND RELEVANCE</u>
are the keys to good counseling.***

<u>Write any additional thoughts here:</u>

ALL KINDS OF *Boxes*

We can assess just how much we are being boxed in at any time.

Some of The Boxes we encounter may not be a relationship issues, such as debt, lack of technical expertise, loss of a job, drinking or drug habits, health problems, taxes, traffic tickets, expensive tastes, eating disorders, etc. Evaluating them is just as important as evaluating relationship issues. The same method can be used. For example, let's examine a health issue:

MY VIEW	DOCTOR'S VIEW
DIRECTIONS: want to live life as usual, and will not want severe eating and activity restrictions. I resent someone who doesn't care I'm happy.	DIRECTIONS: need to go on a special diet and stop playing tennis for awhile -- walking is OK for now -- maybe golf in a few weeks.
REWARDS: the challenge of winning at tennis and having a few beers with the other players is extremely rewarding up an active life.	REWARDS: if you follow the diet carefully and get your back in shape, you may eventually get go back to tennis.

PUNISHMENT: going on a diet ang giving up drinking is awful -- not playing tennis is like giving up an active life.	PUNISHMENT: if you don't diet and keep on like you are, you'll eventually need surgery on. your back, not t mention increasing your high blood pressure.
ENTERTAINMENT: it takes away my weekend and Wednesday night fun to go on a diet and give up tennis with my friends.	ENTERTAINMENT: for a short while by giving up drinking and tennis, you can get back in shape. In the meantime do other things with your friendsor other friends.

As youcan see from this example, there is a great need to negotiate this contract.

STRIVE TO BE HEALTHY

> Health is the foundation to successful parenting
> Emotional and physical health are essential
> Coping in our **boxes** is key for staying healthy
> Finding **healthy boxes** is also key
> It requires effort stay healthy

Healthy parents, healthy kids,

Victimized people usually have a difficult time parenting. It is not that they don't care about parenting properly. They are just too burdened by the emotional load they are carrying, which is often doubled or tripled by their own doubts as parents.

As a parent we can think of our own emotional and physical health as the foundation for our approach to parenting. Just like a foundation of a house, if it crumbles the house also crumbles. Most parents know this, but unfortunately this only adds to the stress they feel about themselves. It can become a vicious cycle of being victimized at work, which causes one to yell at kids, which only adds to the stress as one returns to work. As our own victimization grows, we eventually discover that we are:

CONSTANTLY POINTING THE FINGER AT OUR SELF!

I tend to be hardest on myself if or when:

LIFE IS HUMOROUS

A joyful life is possible if we do not subscribe to **The Box** in our relationships with others. If we use **The Box** to control others, we are constantly busy seeing to it that they "toe the line". If we find ourselves always in **The Box**, we are continually striving to win in it, or at least get better treatment by those using it on us.

REMEMBER – WINNING IN OR WITH
The Box IS NOT SATISFYING!
MAYBE YOUR LIFE CAN BE BASED
ON SOMETHING MORE …

LIVING BEYOND THE BOX!

Living Beyond The Box depends on our understanding of the boxes we find ourselves in. It depends on learning how to cope while we are in them, and how to get out of unhealthy ones. The stress we deal with is largely due to our past and current encounters with ***The Box***.

Not only do we find ourselves in ***The Box,*** we also discover that we use it to control others and to protect ourselves. This only adds to our stress, as those we use it on tend to combat or flea our attempts to control things.

Soon, the collective "we" that defines our lives and various relationships can overwhelm us as we drastically increase the number of boxes and magnify the many consequences that face us. To assert that life today is "far more complex than the good old days" has become a modern "truth".

My hope for all of us is to become more tolerant of one another and to enter an atmosphere of ***Trust and Relevance*** that reduces the debate and competition between us, and increases the negotiation and cooperation needed to live in our face-paced society. I pray we can learn to cope and escape <u>the mounting stress that can hover over us</u> because of ***The Box***.

LIVING BEYOND THE BOX
REDUCES STRESS
AND IMPROVES LIFE !!!

WHAT'S NEXT?
Beyond The Box Guidebooks

1. *Parenting Beyond The Box*
2. *Teaching Beyond The Box*
3. *Counseling Beyond The Box*
4. *Managing Beyond The Box*
5. *Serving Beyond The Box*
6. *Religion Beyond The Box*

As we wrap up our look at **Living Beyond *The Box***, it seems obvious that our lifestyle and living situations carry over into other parts we play. We may find **being caught in *The Box* or using *The Box*** causes us many problems – such as being parents, teachers, coaches, counselors, supervisors, managers, executives, sales representatives, customer service providers, mentors, church leaders, Sunday school teachers, or any other role we try to fill.

The author invites recommendations, ideas, tips and questions that can help him develop **Beyond *The Box* Guidebooks** for the six areas named above. It is planned that those Guidebooks will tackle more specifically the issues of being in *The Box*, using it and getting beyond it for each of those areas. You may contact the author directly to offer input or to ask questions:

Dr. Nelson L. Noggle
EMAIL: *caepnelson@cox.net*

In addition to those Guidebooks, the author is already writing his next complete book entitled:

Acquiring Spiritual Self-Esteem

Printed in the United States
By Bookmasters